THE
PRINCIPLES
OF
RIDING

COMPLETELY REVISED

THE PRINCIPLES OF RIDING

The Official Instruction Handbook of the

GERMAN NATIONAL EQUESTRIAN FEDERATION – BOOK 1

Translated by Christina Belton

KENILWORTH PRESS

First published in Great Britain 1997 by
The Kenilworth Press Ltd
Addington
Buckingham
MK18 2JR

First edition 1985
Enlarged edition 1990
Reprinted in enlarged edition 1991, 1992, 1994, 1996
Completely revised edition 1997
Reprinted 2000, 2001, 2002

British Library Cataloguing in Publication Data
A catalogue record for this book is available from the British Library

ISBN 1-872082-93-9

Translation by Christina Belton
Illustrations by Barbara Wolfgramm (in places by Marianne Merz and Uwe Spenlen)
Design, layout and typesetting by Rachel Howe at Kenilworth Press
Typeset in Frutiger Light 9.5/12.5
Printed in Great Britain by Ebenezer Baylis, Worcester

Acknowledgements

The revision of this volume, and the improvement of specialised sections, was undertaken with
the help of many experts in different fields. Special thanks for ideas and technical information
are due to:

Susanne von Dietze, Angelika Frömming, Isabelle von Neumann-Cosel-Nebe, Helmut Beck-
Broichsitter, Ulrich Conrad, Günther Festerling, Wilfried Gehrmann, Prof. Bodo Hertsch,
Christoph Hess, Dr Reiner Klimke, Dr Gerit Matthesen, Prof Heinz Meyer, Herbert Meyer,
Eckhart Meyners, Prof. Holger Preuschoft, Ralph-Michael Rash, Heinz Schütte, Hans von Scotti,
Hilarius Simons, Paul Stecken, Prof. Dr Gerhard Sybrecht, Konrad Wallner, Hans-Dietmar Wolff.

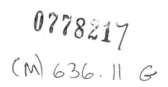

Contents

3. Basic Exercises

4. The Basic Training of the Horse

5. Tips for Riding in Competitions

Preface

The German National Equestrian Federation first published its system of riding and driving forty years ago. There have since been twenty-five editions, and over a quarter of a million copies have been printed. This book is one of six volumes, each being a standard basic textbook on the various subjects – horse knowledge, riding, driving and vaulting – covered by the series.

Based on proven, centuries-old practice, Book 1, *The Principles of Riding* is intended to provide a standardised system of training for schools and clubs giving instruction in riding, and for private training establishments. Horse and rider are trained in accordance with the principles of classical equitation. The following maxims hold true throughout:

- a schooled horse is the best teacher, and
- a young horse should be ridden by an experienced rider.

The basic training described in this book is not intended only as a preparation for competitions and performance tests. On the contrary, it should provide an effective foundation for all forms of equestrian sport. Respecting the correct basic principles ensures that the horse receives a training appropriate to its equine nature, and enables the rider to enjoy his sport and practise it safely.

In this fully revised edition, the content, layout and illustrations have all been changed. There is increased emphasis on the psychological aspects of the horse and rider relationship. Also, the sections on jumping and cross-country training have been expanded and made more comprehensive to reflect the importance of an all-round training.

All six Official Handbooks of the German National Equestrian Federation are essential reading for everyone who rides, drives or trains horses. Moreover, through them the classical principles will be preserved for future generations as a foundation for riding and driving.

German National Equestrian Federation
Sport Section
Warendorf

1 GENERAL

1.1 Equine Nature

An understanding of equine nature is a basic prerequisite for every rider. Only if you try constantly to understand the nature of horses will you be able to act appropriately when you are around them.

The horse is a **herd animal.** The herd unit offers it protection and security. No horse likes to be alone – this is something it has to be introduced to carefully. In training, we can make use of the herd instinct, for example by putting an older, more experienced horse in the lead.

Horses have a **strict 'pecking order',** or herd hierarchy. Rules within the herd society ensure the survival of the herd. Fights to establish the pecking order are part of the horse's instinctive behaviour. They are commonest among youngsters, but are also seen when a new horse is put out in the field. Horses use their feet and teeth to defend themselves. They can be quite ruthless. On the other hand, they show sensitivity in their relationships with each other, and curiosity and affection also feature prominently in their behaviour.

Everyone who rides a horse must be aware that even in horse/human relationships, horses need to establish a pecking order. Only a rider who acts in a calm, firm and logically consistent manner will be accepted by the horse as a higher-ranking being.

Horses are **creatures of flight.** For herbivores, immediate flight offers the best form of protection against all forms of danger. However, different horses have different stimulus thresholds, and any uncertainty or loss of confidence may trigger this flight behaviour. A panicking horse may become oblivious to all outside influences, and as such it can be dangerous.

For the rider, a tendency to shy is an unpleasant consequence of the horse's avoidance-and-flight behaviour. It is pointless to punish the horse for this instinctive reaction. Calm, patient familiarisation with as many new situations as possible will build the horse's confidence and sense of security. In the wild, horses were always **on the move.** In their original habitat, the huge expanses of the steppes, they moved about for many hours of the day finding food. Hence exercise, light, fresh air and contact with other horses are important for the horse's well-being. Special attention must be paid to these criteria when keeping horses in stables, and in their daily care and handling. Horses should be allowed sufficient and varied exercise, and this should include being turned out in a field or exercise area.

Every horse is different in its **character** and **temperament,** likes and dislikes. The horse's moods and intentions can be interpreted through its body language, for example, by its ear or tail movements, or the expression in its eyes (see Section 4.2).

Horses are not naturally aggressive to

those around them, although they are often rough with each other, especially stallions. Handling problems are usually the result of incorrect handling and bad experiences.

The rider must be patient, observant and prepared to spend time learning to interpret the horse's behaviour correctly. Only then will the horse come to have confidence in him and to like him. In time the rider will be able to distinguish between fear and resistance, and to act correctly in his training and education of the horse.

A horse's training is judged not only by the quality of its paces under the rider, but also by whether it has retained its naturalness and individuality.

It is those horses which are contented and ready to give of their best in their day-to-day work which best meet the criteria for a **stable, harmonious relationship between man and horse.** These foundations will be strengthened and developed through patience, psychological understanding and frequent praise.

1.2 The Rider

Handling and riding horses require certain qualities in the rider. These qualities become further established and developed as training progresses. For this reason, riding can be a very valuable character-building exercise, especially for children and young people. Apart from a love for animals and the ability to empathise, patience, self-control, fairness and discipline are required. The rider is responsible for his equine partner. He must be constantly prepared to learn, and he should be ready to look for faults first in himself and not in the horse.

For a rider, being of medium height and a slim build are the ideal but they are not essential for success. All-round fitness is required but the rider does not need to be especially strong. Riding does not demand any exceptional muscle power but it does require good physical coordination. A feel for rhythm and movement are therefore an advantage. More demanding levels of horsemanship require **skill,** strict body control and powers of concentration.

Progress in riding is underpinned by **theoretical knowledge.**

A knowledge of equine nature and behaviour, and of handling and dealing with horses, as well as of equitation and the principles of training, are obvious necessities for any serious, responsible horseman.

Provided that certain ground rules are respected, riding can be very beneficial to health, well-being and the quality of life.

Correct clothing and equipment, especially a hard hat, are important for the rider's **safety.** The horse's bridle and saddle must be in sound condition, and should be checked frequently in order to avoid accidents.

Neglect of established ground rules during schooling, fitness training and in competitions, and also reckless behaviour and underestimating risks, is irresponsible and can lead to potentially dangerous situations.

1.3 The School Horse

A suitable school horse or 'schoolmaster' is one of the most important prerequisites for training the rider.

Ideally, the horse's build should be suited to the rider. However, the height of the horse is not necessarily a factor. A heavy rider should be assigned a strongly built horse (also known as a 'weight carrier'), whereas it may be feasible to use ponies for lighter riders, young people or children.

The school horse should have an equable, calm **temperament** (it should be 'quiet'). Any fear in the rider must first be overcome if he is to go on to develop a supple seat, free from tension and constraint. This quality is known as 'looseness' (German: *Losgelassenheit* – this term is used in connection with both horse and rider). It is easier for the rider to develop confidence on a quiet horse than on an excitable one. However, more advanced students should be given the opportunity to ride lively, sensitive school horses which react to any faults in the rider. This is the best way for the rider to recognise and get to grips with his faults.

A school horse must have undergone a sound **basic education** and be established in its way of going. It should work with looseness *(Losgelassenheit),* and accept the rider's weight and driving aids (it should 'let itself be pushed'). It should come onto the aids easily. A horse which has been schooled and suppled equally on each rein, has a steady contact, and is established in its work, provides the best foundation for learning to ride.

School horses used for **jumping** should have sufficient experience in 'seeing their stride': in other words they should be used to assessing the take-off point without any help. They should always remain calm and not be inclined to become excitable. School horses should be accustomed to being **ridden outdoors.** When riding outside, especially if the riders are inexperienced, only quiet, steady horses should be used.

School horses often work long hours. For this reason, and also because they are ridden by so many different people, they should be treated with care and respect, and they require **careful management** and handling. This should include being ridden by the instructor or another experienced rider in order to check, and if necessary re-establish, their looseness *(Losgelassenheit)* and suppleness (German: *Durchlässigkeit,* or ability to 'let the aids through'). If they are treated correctly and used sensibly, school horses can be kept sound and lead long and useful lives.

The reputation and standing of a riding establishment is based on the quality of its school horses.

1.4 The Instructor

Instructors, also known as trainers, have an especially responsible and varied role in equestrian sport. Riders and horses, with their different aptitudes, have to be trained and improved in accordance with the principles of classical horsemanship, and the riders must at the same time be taught to handle horses safely and appropriately.

This task requires **particularly high levels of practical riding skill and experience,** which should result from riding as many different horses as possible and taking part in different equestrian disciplines. Further qualities required for training horses are discussed in Section 4.1.

The instructor should be willing and able to imagine himself in the student's place so that he can then use his expert knowledge and empathising skills to correct faults and allow the rider to progress.

As well as practical experience and an **aptitude for teaching,** certain character traits are also necessary for this job, for example, a generous, helpful nature, self-control, correctness, enthusiasm and, naturally, a love of horses.

Every instructor and trainer must be aware of the position he holds: he must **set an example** not only in his riding and handling of horses but also personally, in the way he behaves.

Until the basic principles have been learned and have become established, the student needs to have one instructor he can relate to. If the instructor is changed suddenly or too soon, confusion can result.

Advanced riders, and even top-level competition riders, also need to be corrected constantly by experienced professionals in order to combat the faults which can develop only too easily when working unsupervised.

A qualification in instructing, obtained by passing the appropriate examination, should be a 'must' for anyone working as an instructor. In Germany there are qualifications for **amateur** as well as professional instructors. These are obtained by passing graded tests in the various areas of activity, and they lead to different levels of responsibility. However a *Reitwart* (assistant instructor) or *Amateurreitlehrer* (amateur instructor) still needs sufficient skill and knowledge to be able to take a horse through its basic training up to about novice or elementary dressage level (in Germany, classes A/L).

At the end of his training, a student aiming to obtain **professional rider** qualifications takes the nationally recognised *Pferdewirt – Schwerpunkt Reiten* (horsemaster: equitation speciality) examination. After spending a number of years working in the industry, and if he shows the necessary aptitude, he can take the *Pferdewirtschaftsmeister – Schwerpunkt Reiten* examination

(advanced horsemaster: equitation speciality).

As well as being able to give basic training, professional riders who have passed these examinations are also qualified to train riders and horses to higher levels, namely to medium and advanced dressage level (in Germany, classes M/S). They are also the qualified professionals who head the riding and training establishments and bring to them their expertise and high standards.

1.5 The Training Area

The most appropriate place for early training is an indoor school. It is the safest place for the rider while he is not yet fully in control, since it shuts the horse off as far as possible from outside influences which could distract it.

However, the instruction can also be given in a suitable, securely fenced outdoor school. An **open-air riding arena** should, in any case, be available for more advanced training.

Apart from a dressage arena, a **larger training arena** is also desirable, for cantering and galloping work, riding in the light seat and jumping training. There should be sufficient jumps available so that courses can be built regularly. Ideally, practice facilities should also include a natural-looking ditch as well as banks and drop fences.

Once the riders have learned the light, cross-country seat, every attempt should be made to enable them to further develop their skill in an authentic **cross-country setting.** If there is no suitable facility attached to the riding establishment, riders, trainer and horses should be boxed to a suitable location.

The school and the stable yard are the 'showpiece' of any riding establishment. As well as **cleanliness** and **tidiness** in all areas, **care** and **regular maintenance** are obviously essential, for example, the kicking boards in the school and the jumps need to be kept in good condition and the outside track needs to be raked over.

A suitable area should be designated for the **theoretical instruction** which must always accompany the practical training. Some of the theory lessons can take place in the school or in the stable with the horse (e.g. instruction on the conformation of the horse, mane and tail care, bandaging, fitting the saddle and bridle, etc.). **Demonstration material** should be used as much as possible. Training films or the use of a camcorder will make the instruction more interesting and meaningful.

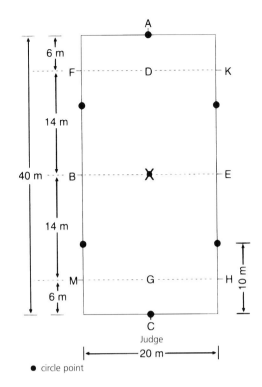

20 x 40m dressage arena, used for novice tests.

1.6 The School

Arena markers

To help prevent misunderstandings, a standardised system of arena markers and rules is used.

An arena used for dressage competitions can be either 20m x 40m or 20m x 60m. A 20m x 40m arena is usually used for basic training, and is also used for most dressage tests up to elementary level (in Germany, for classes E/A/L).

The markers are as follows:
* The letters A and C mark the middle of the two short sides.
* The letters B and E (also known as the 'half markers') are found in the middle of the long sides.

* The markers M, F, K and H are on the long sides, 6m from the ends of the arena. D and G are level with these, on the centre line.

In addition to these, the 'circle points' (shown on the diagram with a black dot) are the points where the 20m circle in each half of the arena touches the sides. The circle points on the long sides are also known as the 'quarter markers'.

The centre point of the arena is known as 'X'. It is also the seventh circle point.

A code of practice ensures that riders in exercise areas and schools can practise and train together without getting in each other's way. Every rider needs to be familiar with the following rules:

* Before entering the school or opening the door, the person entering always checks that the door can be opened safely by calling **'Door clear',** and waiting until he hears **'Door clear'** in reply. The same applies when leaving the school.

* **Mounting and dismounting,** as well as halting in order to tighten the girth etc., always take place in the centre of a circle or on the centre line.

* An adequate **safety distance** of at least three steps (about 2.5m) must be kept in front and to the side of each horse.

* Riders **walking** their horses or halting must leave the outside track free for riders in trot and canter. Downward transitions to walk or halt should be performed only on an inside track.

* Riders on a circle must give way to riders on the outside track: the outside track has priority over the circle.

* If there is riding in both directions (i.e. **on both reins**), the riders on the right rein must give way. The riders on the left

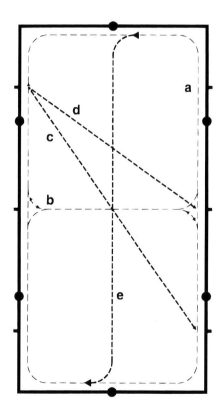

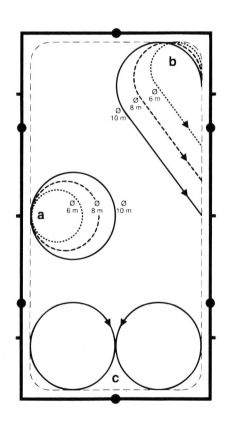

a Going large (outside track).
b Change of rein across the centre of the school.
c and **d** Turning diagonally across the school.
e Change of rein down the centre line.

a 6m volte, 8m and 10m circles.
b Half volte/half circle (in the corner) and return to track (change of rein through the half volte).
c Figure of eight.

rein have priority on the track.

* If the riders are all on the same rein and the command is given to **change the rein,** once the riders reach the track after changing the rein, they are entitled to remain on the track. Riders who have yet to perform the change of rein must give way by moving inwards.

* **Lungeing** in the exercise area or in the school may only take place with the agreement of all the riders present. Lungeing should not be allowed whilst a lesson is in progress or when more than three riders are training simultaneously.

* **Jumps** or parts of jumps should be stored outside the school or arena when not in use. If they are to remain temporarily in the arena, they should be tidily arranged in the middle of the school.

The school figures

The school figures are set out in the following diagrams.

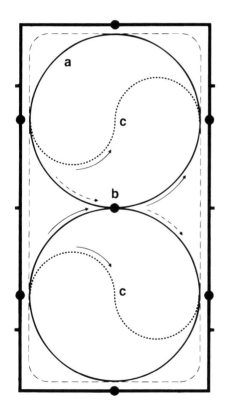

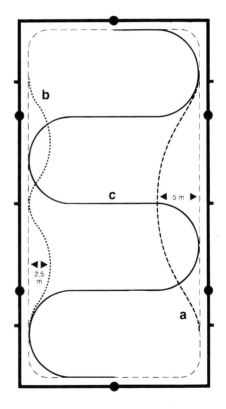

a Circle.
b Change of rein out of the circle.
c Change of rein through the circle.

a One-loop serpentine on the long side.
b Two-loop on the long side.
c Four-loop serpentine across the whole school.

1.7 Code of Practice for Hacking Out and Cross-Country Riding

Riding outdoors plays an important part in the rider's basic training. Apart from having a secure seat, the rider needs to be familiar with the basic code of conduct for riding in the countryside.

As a **visitor** to the countryside he must always behave in such a way that he makes only friends, not enemies. Not all riders are lucky enough to have 'riding country' right outside the stables, with no busy roads to cross. It is in the rider's own interest to keep the dangers and risks of riding outside to a minimum.

Horses which are used for hacking and cross-country work by less experienced riders must receive sufficient exercise each day, and be accustomed to traffic, otherwise potentially dangerous situations can arise. As a means of minimising tension, and so that the girths can be tightened, the horses should be ridden for a while in the school beforehand to loosen them up.

The rider must wear an appropriate **hard hat** (safety helmet) with a harness and correct footwear (boots or jodhpur boots).

For **safety** reasons, the condition, fit and suitability of the tack must be checked before each ride.

Inexperienced riders should never ride out alone. They should always be accompanied by someone experienced or be properly escorted by a qualified member of staff.

Horses should always be ridden in walk on concrete or tarmac **roads and tracks,** to avoid damaging their legs and because of the risk of slipping.

The rider should avoid gullies, banks, footpaths and cycle tracks because they are susceptible to damage by horses' feet, as are paths made soft by rain or frost.

The **pace** must be suited to the situation and the conditions. Walkers, cyclists, other riders and motor vehicles should be passed in walk.

When riding on field and woodland tracks, the gait and pace depend on the following:
* the surface
* weather conditions
* whether you can see clearly what lies ahead
* the rider's level of training
* the horse's level of training.

If any unforeseen damage is done during the ride, it must be reported immediately to the owner of the land so that compensation can be agreed.

As a means of **communicating** intentions to the rest of the group, and for the benefit of other people using the path or road, the following hand signals are used by the lead rider then repeated by the other riders:

* Hand raised and held: means slow down to walk or halt.

* Several short upward movements of the hand: means catch up, trot on or canter on, as specified beforehand by the lead rider.

* Changes of direction on public roads and tracks are indicated by an outstretched right or left arm as appropriate.

The rider bringing up the rear gives the same signal, for the benefit of other users of the track.

Riders may ride in pairs (with a distance of about 2.5m between them) if the path is wide enough and if this will not disturb other users. The first canter should follow several periods of walk and trot during which the horses have had a chance to loosen up properly.

Each ride should be beneficial to the horse's training and, since it entails being out in the fresh air and in a rural environment, it should also be a **recreational** experience for the rider and serve to promote the horse's **well-being.** However, safety is the primary consideration for all those taking part. The demands should therefore be pitched at the level of the least experienced rider. The saying 'a chain is only as strong as its weakest link' is especially true of outdoor group rides.

1.8 Dress and Equipment

Dress

For early lessons the novice rider simply needs to wear something tough and comfortable. Riding boots are not required at this stage, but shoes must have a proper heel to prevent the foot inadvertently slipping through the stirrup. For safety reasons, an approved riding hat is essential from the outset.

Once past the initial stages, proper riding wear is recommended. Particularly important are well-fitting **riding breeches or jodhpurs.** These should not be too tight across the knee and should have no tendency to wrinkle in the areas in contact with the saddle, since this could cause sores. They should be cut generously enough not to be tight at the crotch. The **boots** should be high enough – low-cut boots can catch on the saddle flap and

interfere with the rider's seat and aids. The boots should have a 'through sole', which finishes at the heel. A short sole is not safe since the back edge can catch on the stirrup, trapping the foot. This also applies to jodhpur boots, which are worn with jodhpurs rather than breeches.

It is a good idea to wear suitable **gloves.** These should not be too tight across the back of the hand or they will interfere with the rider's 'feel' and will not protect the hand from the cold in winter. If wool or 'string' gloves are used, leather patches between the third and little fingers and between the thumb and index finger will improve the grip and help to prevent the reins from slipping through the fingers.

A hard, 'unbreakable', shatter-proof **riding hat or a jockey skull cap** with a safety harness, to the latest safety standards, is indispensable for all riders! (If competing, it is advisable to check on the requirements of the competition rules.)

A **whip** of about 1.1m to 1.2m is recommended, especially for novice riders, whose aids are still rather ineffectual. It should be firm enough not to keep flexing and tapping the horse unintentionally in time with the stride. On the other hand, it should be flexible enough to allow the rider to use it accurately and positively with only small movements of his hand. A short jumping whip, no longer than 75cm, is recommended for jumping and riding out.

Spurs should not be worn by novice riders except on the instructor's recommendation. Spurs are attached horizontally about four to five finger widths above the heel. If the spurs are fitted with rowels, these must turn freely to prevent injury to the horse. Particular attention should be paid to this point when the horse is changing coat.

To begin with, a **riding jacket** is not essential for a novice rider. When one is

Safety hat with
harness

Riding boot

Riding gloves

Spur

Jumping whip

Dressage whip

Jockey skull
cap

Jockey skull cap with
silk cover

acquired, it should be wide enough across the shoulders not to restrict the rider's freedom of movement, and not so long that it can get caught underneath his seat when he sits down. If a sweater or shirt is worn, it should not be too loose or it will hide the rider's position and prevent the instructor from being able to correct it.

Saddlery

The basic equipment consists of the **bridle** (snaffle or double bridle) and the **saddle.**
Further equipment and **auxiliary aids** consist of side-reins, other types of auxiliary reins, martingales, bandages, boots, breastplates and foregirths.

The snaffle bridle

The snaffle is the most suitable bridle for

basic training, be it flatwork, jumping or riding out. It is made up of two parts:
* the basic bridle, the bit and the reins
* the noseband.

The basic bridle consists of the headpiece, cheekpieces, throatlatch and browband. The size of the bridle can be adjusted at the buckle attached to one or both of the cheekpieces. Buckles on the headpiece (on top of the horse's poll) are dangerous for the rider.

The **snaffle bit** acts on the horse's tongue and the bars of the mouth. As a general rule, the thinner the bit, the more severe its action. A thick mouthpiece, provided it is not too thick to fit comfortably in the mouth, is readily accepted by most horses. The bit (or the two bits in the case of a double bridle) lies on the bars, the space in the lower jaw where there are no teeth.

Snaffle bits differ not only in their thickness but also in their shape and cross-section. They can be single-jointed, i.e. with a joint or hinge in the middle, or double-jointed, i.e. with two joints. The better the bit fits the mouth, the more it encourages the horse to mouth it. Bits which correspond to the shape of the horse's mouth are the best fit and the most comfortable.

The outer end of the mouthpiece of a snaffle, measured at the corners of the mouth, should be a minimum of 14mm thick. As a rule, bits come in sizes ranging from 12.5cm to 15cm (smaller for ponies), at 5mm spacings. The length must always correspond to the width of the mouth. If the bit is too narrow, it will pinch the corners of the horse's mouth. If it is too wide, it will slide from side to side and be unsteady in the mouth. Also, the two sides of the mouthpiece, if too long, can squeeze the lower jaw, causing a 'nutcracker' effect. There is also a risk that the horse will put its tongue over the bit. There should be no worn parts, sharp edges or patches of rust, since these could

Position of the bit in the mouth.

cause injury to the horse's mouth.

For riding, the following types of snaffle are usually used:

The **loose-ring snaffle** is the most common bit and is used both on young horses and in more advanced training, because it has a mild action while still providing an effective means of control. The mouthpiece can be either hollow and light, or solid and therefore heavier. A heavy bit has the advantage that it stays stiller in the mouth so that it gives the horse less encouragement to play with it with its tongue.

Snaffle bridle with drop noseband.

1 Headpiece
2 Cheekpiece
3 Throatlatch
4 Browband
5 Noseband
6 Chinstrap
7 Snaffle bit
8 Rein
9 Martingale stop

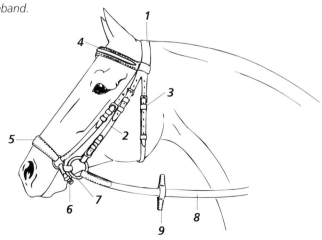

Single-jointed loose-ring snaffle

Double-jointed loose-ring snaffle (French snaffle)

Single-jointed eggbutt snaffle

Double-jointed eggbutt snaffle

Cheek snaffle

Loose-ring snaffles can be either single-jointed or double-jointed. The single-jointed snaffle is the most commonly used bit. The double-jointed snaffle has the advantage that, with its two joints and middle section, it follows the contours of the mouth particularly well.

The **eggbutt snaffle** differs from the loose-ring snaffle in having rings the shape of a rounded 'D', which are hinged onto the mouthpiece. Used as a temporary measure, this type of bit has been found to give good results on horses with sensitive mouths since it tends to lie stiller in the mouth.

The **cheek snaffle** has bars on each side and can be used on horses which are difficult to turn. The bars, or 'cheeks', are positioned on each side of the horse's mouth and prevent the bit from being pulled through the mouth, which would lead to loss of control. A similar effect can be achieved by fitting rubber rings onto a loose-ring snaffle. The cheek snaffle also has loose rings thus ensuring free movement of the jointed mouthpiece.

Horses which have a tendency to roll their tongues up when being ridden can be fitted (as a temporary measure) with a bit which has a special, high port (a tongue depressor bit). However, tongue problems are almost always due to using the hands too strongly and/or to tension in the horse. Improving the horse's suppleness and keeping the contact soft is the best way to tackle this problem. It is also important that the bit fits exactly and is correctly adjusted.

> **NOTE**   As a basic principle, a more severe bit will not compensate for lack of suppleness. The effects of bad hands are simply exaggerated by severe bits.

It can sometimes help to change the type of bit and the material it is made of. Many horses will accept a rubber or synthetic bit more readily than a metal one. Information on the types of bit allowed in competitions can be found in the appropriate rule books.

The **reins,** which are usually made of leather or webbing, are either buckled or sewn onto the bit rings or attached by hook-stud fasteners, and are buckled together at their other ends. The length of the two reins together is approximately 2.75m and they are about 2cm wide. Webbing reins have the advantage of

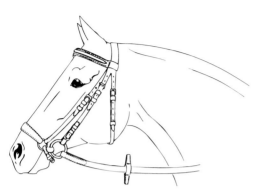

Drop noseband

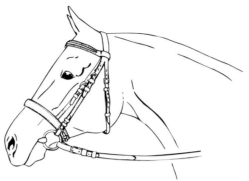

Cavesson noseband

being less likely to slip through the hands when wet. Additional grip can be provided by leather strips sewn onto the reins. The quality of the leather or webbing, of the buckles or studs and of the stitching, is important for safety reasons.

The noseband completes the bridle. It keeps the top and bottom jaws in alignment. A correctly adjusted noseband (not too tight but not too loose either) serves to lighten the pressure of the bit on the bars by indirectly transferring some of its action onto the nasal bone. It also prevents the horse evading the rein aids by opening its mouth. The type of noseband depends on the horse, and should be chosen with the help of the instructor.

On the **drop noseband** the nosepiece is a bit wider in the centre than at the sides. It has a small ring at each end to which the chinstrap and the head piece are attached. The nosepiece must be short enough for the rings not to press on the bit in any circumstances. The nosepiece should rest on the bony part of the nose, about four fingers' widths above the top edge of the nostril.

The chin strap is fastened below the bit and adjusted so that there is approximately room for two fingers between it and the jaw bones. It should never restrict the horse's breathing.

The **cavesson noseband** has a wider, more substantial nosepiece. In Germany it is used primarily with a double bridle. It fits above the bit(s) and is adjusted so that it lies just below the bottom of the cheek bone and does not press on it.

Examples of other types of noseband based on these two basic types are the flash noseband and the combination noseband.

The **flash noseband** consists of a cavesson noseband with a loop on the front. A narrower strap runs through this loop and round the horse's jaws below the bit. To prevent it being pulled downwards, the top part of the noseband should always be fastened before the bottom strap.

This noseband works well on horses which have good mobility in their mouths and are sufficiently supple (i.e. prepared to 'let the aids through').

The **combination noseband** consists of a nosepiece with a horseshoe-shaped piece of metal attached to each end. An upper and a lower chinstrap are attached, one to each end of the horseshoe shape.

The metal piece restricts the sideways movement of the horse's jaw. Also, if the noseband is correctly adjusted, it does not interfere with the bit rings, which in some cases encourages the horse to move its mouth more freely.

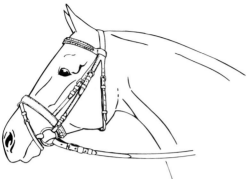

Flash noseband

Combination noseband

The **Grakle noseband** consists of two straps which cross over the nasal bone and are held together on the nose by a padded leather disc. Its action is similar to that of the flash noseband except that, if correctly adjusted, it has the advantage of being well clear of the nostrils, so that it cannot interfere with the horse's breathing. It is for this reason that it is used primarily on event horses. It is particularly important that it is correctly adjusted so that the upper strap does not press on the bottom of the cheek bone.

When used by an experienced rider on a suitably schooled horse, the **double bridle** permits a more refined use of the aids.

The rider must first have learned to ride basic dressage (up to elementary/German Class L standard) correctly in a snaffle.

The double bridle as used for trained dressage horses consists of two bits so that the rider has two sets of reins to handle at once. The **bridoon** can be either of the loose-ring type (single- or double-jointed) or an eggbutt. It is thinner than the normal snaffle (minimum 10mm) and is attached to a separate headpiece which lies underneath that of the curb bit.

The **curb bit** is a straight bar (unjointed) bit with cheeks (lever arms) at the sides. The cheeks and the curb chain work together. The length of the cheeks determines the severity of the bit: the shorter the cheeks, the milder is the lever action. A curb with long cheeks exercises a more powerful effect but works more slowly. As a rule, the mouthpiece of the curb is about 0.5cm shorter than that of the bridoon because the latter lies in a slightly bent position in the mouth owing to its joint or joints. However, a slightly wider curb bit may be more appropriate if the horse has fleshy lips.

The action of the curb bit is also influenced by the so-called 'port' and by the thickness of the mouthpiece. The port is the upward bend in the centre of the mouthpiece. The higher the port, the more it permits the tongue to fit into it and

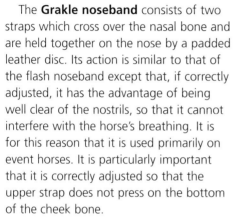

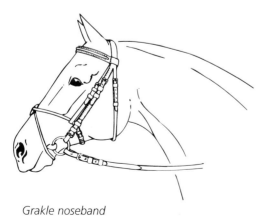

Grakle noseband

Double bridle

1 Cavesson noseband
2 Cheekpiece of curb bit
3 Cheekpiece of bridoon bit
4 Snaffle rein
5 Curb rein
6 Bridoon bit
7 Curb bit
8 Curb chain

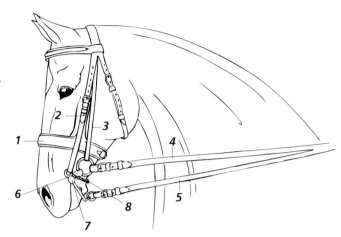

consequently the more the sides of the mouthpiece act on the bars of the mouth.

The length of the upper and lower cheeks should be in the ratio of 1:1.5 to 1:2.

In Germany, in competitions and performance tests, the length of the cheeks is laid down in the rules. In dressage tests the length should be 5-10cm, while 7cm is the maximum for all other disciplines in which curb bits are allowed. (Note: in other countries different measurements may be stipulated.) In performance tests, the mouthpiece of the curb must be a minimum of 14mm thick, measured at the corners of the mouth.

The cheekpieces of the bridle are attached to the upper cheeks of the curb and the reins to the movable rings on the lower cheeks. The curb reins should be slightly narrower than the bridoon reins.

The **curb chain** consists of oval rings, tapering towards the ends of the chain and shaped so that they can lie flat on top of each other. Half way along the curb chain there is a small ring through which the **lip strap** is passed. The latter is attached at each end to an eye in the bottom half of each of the lower cheeks; it regulates the position (height) of the curb chain. It also prevents the horse catching hold of the cheeks of the bit with its teeth.

Curb bit

Bridoon bit

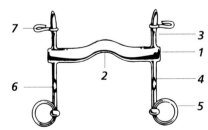

Curb chain

1 Mouthpiece
2 Port
3 Upper cheek
4 Lower cheek
5 Ring
6 Eye for lip strap
7 Curb hook

The **curb hooks** are twisted outwards, with the opening at the front. (Note: in other countries the opening tends to be at the back. This also affects whether it is hooked on from the inside or the outside – see below.) The curb chain, which is always twisted clockwise, is hooked on from the top: from the outside on the left side and from the inside on the right. If it does not lie flat, its action and that of the bit will not be correct. Also, distorted or wrongly bent curb hooks can cause mouth injuries.

A cavesson noseband is used with a double bridle.

Other bits and bridles

The various types of **pelham** and the **hackamore** count as specialised bits and bridles and should be used only for specific purposes and by experienced riders. They require an independent seat and good hands.

In Germany, the **pelham** is usually of the jointed type so that it looks like a snaffle with the cheeks of a curb and a curb chain. It has a lever action similar to that of the curb. Leather couplings ('roundings') can be fitted from the top to the bottom ring to allow the bit to be used with only one set of reins.

The **hackamore** is a bitless bridle which acts on the nose, the chin groove and the poll. Hackamores are used primarily in Western riding.

The purpose of the hackamore is to act

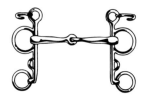

Jointed pelham

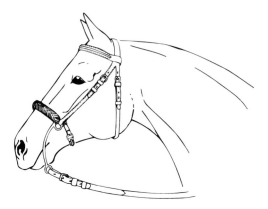

Hackamore

on areas other than the mouth. However, bitless bridles are not necessarily more pleasant for the horse, since they can be very severe if wrongly used. For this reason, hackamores should be used only by experienced riders capable of using the reins very sensitively. In Germany, use of the hackamore is permitted in jumping competitions at novice level.

Saddles

Each saddle is made up of the following parts:

The **tree** determines the shape of the saddle. It may be made out of steel, leather, whale bone or a synthetic material.

The **pommel** is built on the slightly raised, sometimes backward-sloping arch at the front of the tree. It must be high enough to prevent at all times (including when the rider's weight is in the saddle) any pressure on the long spinous processes of the vertebrae which lie just under the skin. The height of the pommel is determined by the height of the withers.

The **cantle** is the rearmost part of the seat of the saddle.

The **panels** contain the padding between the tree and the horse's back. This padding is usually made of horse-hair

Parts of the saddle

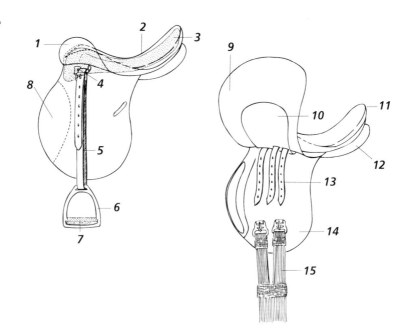

1 Pommel
2 Seat
3 Tree
4 Stirrup bar
5 Stirrup leather
6 Stirrup
7 Stirrup tread
8 Knee roll
9 Saddle flap
10 Buckle guard
11 Cantle
12 Panel
13 Girth tabs
14 Sweat flap
15 Girth

or tow. It must not be lumpy or compressible and should be no thicker than absolutely necessary.

Knee rolls are the thicker sections of padding which are usually found underneath the saddle flaps but may be on their front upper edge.

The shape of the **seat** has an important influence on the position of the rider. The deepest point of the seat should be in the centre of the saddle.

The **saddle flaps** form the sides of the saddle. Their shape depends on the type of saddle, i.e. whether it is a dressage, jumping or general-purpose saddle. The leather used must be firm and of the best quality.

The **girth tabs or girth straps** are the straps to which the girth is attached. For safety reasons, the best ones are hand sewn and made from tough, almost unbreakable leather (chrome leather).

The **girth** must be fairly wide so as to provide a large enough surface in contact with the horse. Forged buckles are

preferable to cast iron or nickel. Girths are made of cord, leather or synthetic material and may have elastic inserts.

The **stirrup leathers** should be made from supple, hard-wearing leather. The buckle should be sewn on by hand and about 7cm of leather should be passed through the buckle and sewn down. Oval holes make it easier to adjust the stirrups.

The **stirrup bar** holds the stirrup onto the saddle. It has a **safety catch or 'thumb piece'** on the end, which is designed to open and release the leather in the event of a fall. The hinge should obviously be kept well oiled though it is usually left open.

The **stirrup** must be wide enough (approximately 12cm for adults and 10cm for children) and heavy enough so that the rider can pick it up and release it from his foot easily. Rubber treads can be used to provide extra grip. The slot for the stirrup leather should be smooth so as not to damage the leather.

The purpose of a **numnah** is to prevent

sweat coming into contact with the lining of the saddle. Numnahs are made of cotton, felt, leather, rubber and synthetic material. They are either shaped to the saddle or are rectangular (e.g. 'saddle cloths'). Folded woollen blankets and other extra padding should only be used in special cases since they prevent the rider from sitting close to the horse. However, they offer a useful means of protecting the horse's back when out trekking or when using a Western or army-type saddle.

Types of saddle

The rider can sit and give the aids correctly only if he is seated in a correctly constructed, well-fitting saddle.

There are two main types of saddle:
* the modern sports saddle, based on the English hunting saddle, and
* the Western or army-style saddle.

The modern **sports saddle** is characterised by its one-piece tree, its closeness to the horse and its light weight. It is this type of saddle which is used for training and in equestrian sport.

There are three different styles:
* The **dressage saddle,** which fits close to the horse's back and has long flaps.

* The **jumping saddle,** which is longer in

the seat and has forward-cut flaps, and possibly more substantial knee-rolls.

* The **general-purpose saddle,** which is half-way between the dressage and the jumping saddle in style. It is suitable for basic dressage as well as jumping and cross-country riding. It is the saddle of choice for novice riders and for the basic training of the horse.

When checking the fit of a saddle (which is best done without a numnah), it is especially important to ensure that it has an even contact all over with the horse's back. The lowest point must be in the centre of the seat. The pommel must be high enough to prevent contact with the withers when the rider's weight is in the saddle. If the saddle does not meet these criteria, a different saddle should be tried or the original one restuffed if this is feasible.

A badly fitting saddle can cause injuries which do not heal easily and which entail long periods off work.

Auxiliary reins and martingales

These are used in the training of novice riders to compensate for their (as yet) not fully effective use of the aids and to make it easier for them to understand what is required. Correctly adjusted side-reins, for example, will cause the horse to lower its

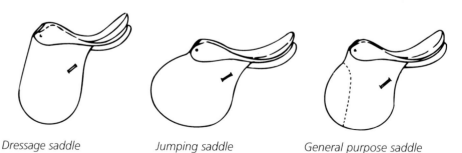

Dressage saddle   Jumping saddle   General purpose saddle

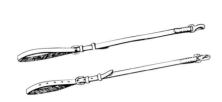

Side-reins

Double side-reins (running reins)

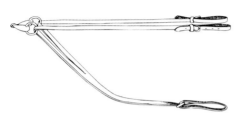

Triangular pattern side-reins

Running martingale

head and neck and soften its back, so that the young rider can experience and learn to ride with a correct, supple seat.

The main auxiliary reins and martingales used in basic training are:
* side-reins (single)
* triangular pattern side-reins
* double side-reins (running reins)
* running martingale
* German standing martingale.

Side-reins (single) are two narrow leather or webbing straps about 1.2 to 1.5m long. At one end is a buckle or spring clip which attaches to the bit ring, while at the other end there is a large loop, adjustable by means of a buckle, which attaches to the saddle or lungeing roller. There should be enough holes to allow the reins to be adjusted to whatever length is required.

   Triangular pattern side-reins consist of a strap 2.5 to 2.75m long which divides into two part of the way along its length. At both ends there are adjustable loops which attach to the girth. The wide end

is attached to the girth between the horse's forelegs, then the divided ends are passed through the bit rings (from the inside to the outside) and back to the girth. In both triangular pattern and double side-reins, the side pair of loops (the top pair on the triangular pattern reins and the bottom pair on the double side-reins) are usually attached to the girth underneath the saddle flaps. They must not be allowed to slip down behind the elbows.

   Double side-reins (also known as running reins) are used primarily for lungeing and they are better attached to a lungeing roller than to a saddle. When used on the latter they should be attached to the 'D's just below the pommel. The reins are each about 2.25m long. They run through the bit rings, from the inside to the outside, and back to the girth, where they are attached in about the same position as single side-reins.

   The **running martingale** is made up of a strap with a loop at one end which is attached to the girth, whilst at the other

German standing martingale

end it splits into two pieces, each with a ring at the end. The snaffle reins are threaded through these rings. A neck strap with a rubber ring at the bottom keeps the martingale in position, and 'martingale stops' on the reins prevent the rings from catching on the rein fastenings near the bit. The martingale should be long enough not to exert any pressure on the reins when the horse's head and neck position are normal. As a rough guide to the length, the rings should be level with the point of the hip.

The **German standing martingale** should be used with caution since it has the undesirable effect of encouraging the horse to use, and so develop, the muscles on the underside of its neck. This type of martingale consists of a single side-rein attached to the girth between the horse's forelegs and clipped onto a coupling attached to the rings of the snaffle.

Any pull on the coupling draws the two sides of the bit together, which can cause the lower jaw to be pinched and the joint of the bit to dig into the roof of the horse's mouth.

Accessories

Bandages and boots protect the horse's legs from external injury, for example, from 'brushing' or knocks from jumps. They can be used to protect the fore- and hind legs of young horses which have not yet found their balance and for lunge work and loose jumping. However, they are also suitable for use on older horses.

Bandages are about 1.8 to 3m long and 10 to 15cm wide. They are made of wool, cotton or an elasticated material such as crepe.

Bandages must be correctly fitted so as to avoid restricting the blood supply or the movement, or causing pressure injuries. When riding in deep, sandy going, grains of sand may work their way underneath the bandages and cause sores and inflammation. Bandages should be neither too loose nor too tight and should be flat and wrinkle-free.

Bandaging over padding, e.g. gamgee tissue, helps to prevent these problems.

When securing bandages with tapes, the tapes must not be tighter than the

Bandages

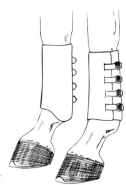

Brushing boots

bandage. However, the bow used to tie the tapes must be tight, so that it cannot come undone. The ends of the tape should be tucked in behind the bandage. Bandages with velcro fastenings are the easiest to use.

Brushing boots are used on both the fore- and the hind feet and are made of felt, leather, or most commonly a synthetic material. They are usually lined with foam rubber. Normally, they fasten on the outside of the leg, from front to back. **Fetlock boots** are used primarily for jumping and outdoor riding. They protect the fetlock joints of the hind legs and are fitted as described above.

Overreach boots or **bell boots** (USA) are pulled on over the foot and protect the sensitive coronary band and the bulbs of the heels. They prevent the hind feet from striking into the hollow of the heels of the forefeet.

If the horse has a badly shaped back and withers, or flat withers, a **breastplate,** a **foregirth** or a **crupper** may be helpful.

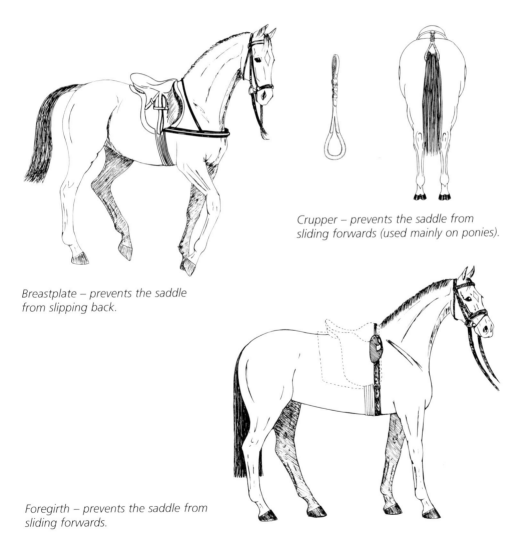

Crupper – prevents the saddle from sliding forwards (used mainly on ponies).

Breastplate – prevents the saddle from slipping back.

Foregirth – prevents the saddle from sliding forwards.

Care of saddlery

Good quality saddlery is a very expensive item but, if given regular, knowledgeable care and stored correctly, it will last for a long time.

All saddlery should be:
* cleaned every time it is used,
* treated with leather care preparations, especially around the stitching, every 8 to 14 days depending on use,
* regularly inspected thoroughly for damage, especially to movable parts and stitching,
* on top of this, all the equipment should be 'spring cleaned' about twice yearly.

In the **daily cleaning** after use, the metal parts should be washed with water and then finished off with a cloth. Care must be taken to keep the water off any attached leather parts such as reins etc. Leather parts should be wiped over with a cloth or sponge to remove the dirt, then saddle soap should be applied to the top surface.

   To apply **leather-care preparations,** first clean the leather thoroughly (bridles etc. should obviously have been completely taken apart beforehand), then apply the leather dressing or oil. If the leatherwork does not come into direct contact with the horse, or is supposed to retain a measure of stiffness (such as saddle flaps), a thin layer of a leather dressing should be applied and then worked in by hand. Leatherwork which comes in contact with the horse, such as saddle linings etc., should be treated with (leather care) oil. This should also be applied sparingly. Leather needs moisture to prevent it cracking and leather-care preparations are designed to keep the leather moist. Oil keeps the leather supple, but if used too frequently it weakens the texture of the leather and makes it flabby.

* Chrome leather and smooth leather reins should not be treated with greasy leather dressings.
* Buckles or metal parts should be oiled very sparingly.
* Stirrups and other large, visible metal parts such as bits and curb chains can be cleaned with metal polish.
* The mouthpiece of the bit should not be allowed to come in contact with chemical cleaning agents.
* Rubber and suede should be wiped over with a damp cloth or sponge.
* Wool and linen bandages should be washed with washing powder.

Stitching which is coming undone should be repaired promptly, and metal parts with cracks or sharp edges (bits, for example) should be replaced immediately.

   Spring cleaning entails taking apart all the leather parts and thoroughly cleaning them with luke-warm water and the appropriate cleaning materials, then leaving them to dry away from direct heat. Only when dry should they be treated with leather preparations as described above.

   Saddlery and equipment, especially leatherwork, should be **stored** in a dust-free room which is not too dry and which can be heated in winter. Mildew formation can be prevented by good ventilation and occasionally wiping the equipment over with a cloth.

   Bridles should be hung up and saddles stored on saddle racks or poles. Saddles should be handled with special care to avoid damaging the tree. Items of equipment not in regular use can be given a more generous coating of leather dressing or oil and hung up out of the way.

1.9 Preparations for Riding

Care of the horse

The horse's performance and well-being are greatly influenced by its stabling, feeding and care. These subjects are dealt with in Horse Management, in the same series. However, every rider must have essential basic knowledge in these areas.

The aim of **daily grooming** is to remove dust, dirt and waste products such as scurf and sweat from the hair and skin. Grooming also serves to massage the skin and stimulate the circulation in the skin and connective tissue, and it helps the skin to 'breathe'. Hence, grooming is not simply a cleaning process; it is also beneficial to the horse's health and makes an important contribution to the horse's well-being and performance.

In the **natural environment** these effects are achieved through mutual grooming and by rolling and scratching. For horses living outside, formal grooming could even be harmful since a certain build-up of grease and dust is necessary to protect the horse against the weather.

In the **artificial environment of the stable,** it is man who is responsible for grooming and caring for the horse. The **grooming kit** consists of a body brush, curry comb, dandy brush, water brush, stable rubbers, sponges, mane comb and hoof pick. Electric grooming machines are a worthwhile investment for larger establishments, where they save time and energy. The horse is taken either outside or into the stable corridor to be groomed. **Tying** the horse on each side, with a rope or plastic covered chain, will prevent misbehaviour. The rope or chain must be easy to release at both ends, for example, by means of a special quick-release clip

('**panic clip'**) and a **'halter knot',** which can be undone even when under tension, i.e. if the horse pulls back.

First, the coat is gently scuffed with a curry comb to remove hard crusts of dirt. It must not be used on areas where there is no layer of flesh, such as the head, limbs and points of the hip.

Next, the horse is cleaned with the **body brush**, starting at the head and working with the lie of the hair. After each stroke, the brush is passed over the curry comb, which is tapped on the ground from time to time to remove the dust. To finish off, the horse is wiped with a cloth (stable rubber) to remove the last traces of dust.

The corners of the eyes, the nostrils, the sides of the mouth, the underside of the tail and the anus must be washed as required with a **sponge.** Separate sponges should be used for the head and the tail, and they should be washed frequently and thoroughly in hot water.

In warm weather the horse can be carefully washed down after strenuous exercise. Sponging over the saddle patch in particular is good for the horse and makes grooming easier.

Mane and tail care

The **tail** should be worked through daily with the fingers. Brushes and combs should not be used on the tail itself because they pull out too many hairs. The tail can be washed as required with warm water and perhaps with a suitable shampoo. The mane is combed with a mane comb or brushed flat with a damp brush.

In normal conditions the use of **rugs** in the stable makes horses 'soft' and lowers their resistance to colds. However, for horses which grow a particularly thick winter coat or which sweat a lot when working, clipping and rugging up may be preferable, since otherwise in cold, wet weather the coat takes a long time to dry out and the horse is at greater risk of catching cold.

Putting on the bridle

If the horse is in a stable the bridle is put on before the saddle. If the horse is in a stall or tied up outside the stable, it makes more sense to put the saddle on first.

To put on a **snaffle bridle,** first arrange the bridle correctly and hold it in your left hand. Then:

* Approach the horse from the left.

* With the horse standing calmly, pass the reins over its head with your right hand.

* With your right hand on the nasal bone, remove the headcollar.

* Put your right hand back around the

Putting on the bridle.

horse's nose, and transfer the bridle to it from your left hand.

* Hold the bit in the flat of your left hand and position it ready to go into the horse's mouth.

* Press your thumb gently on the lips to open the horse's mouth.

* At the same time carefully lift the bridle so that the bit is drawn slowly into the horse's mouth without banging against the teeth.

* With your right hand lift the headpiece as high as it will go, and pull it first over one ear then over the other, using your left hand, which is now free, to help if necessary.

* Pull the forelock out so that it lies on top of the browband, and tidy the mane from under the headpiece.

* Finally, fasten the throatlatch and noseband.

The bridle is correctly adjusted when the bit is high enough to touch the corners of the horse's mouth and to cause two wrinkles, but no more, to form on each side. The headpiece should lie just behind the ears, but without chafing them – hence the browband needs to be of adequate length. The throatlatch should be loose enough to allow a hand held on its side to fit between it and the horse's throat.

The drop noseband should lie about four finger-widths above the nostrils and should be adjusted so that the horse has room to mouth the bit in comfort but not to open its mouth wide enough to constitute a resistance. The rings joining the nosepiece to the chinstrap should be in front of the mouthpiece of the bit. If they are further back, this means that the nosepiece is too long. The chinstrap should fasten in the chin groove, with the buckle on the outside of the jawbone so that it does not press on it. The top edge of the nosepiece of the cavesson noseband, or of the cavesson part of the flash noseband, should lie one finger's width below the bottom of the cheekbone, and the noseband should be adjusted so that there is room for at least one finger to be inserted between it and the nasal bone.

A **double bridle** is fitted in the same way as a snaffle. Special care should be taken when pulling the unjointed curb bit into the horse's mouth.

On a double bridle:
* The bridoon should be the same height in the horse's mouth as a snaffle.

* The width of the curb should be such that there is about half a centimetre of the mouthpiece showing on each side between the corner of the mouth and the cheek of the bit. Curb bits which are too wide slide sideways and then act only on one side, i.e. on one of the bars. Bits which are too narrow chafe the lips. The mouthpiece of the curb should lie underneath that of the bridoon. It should not be low enough to come in contact with the tushes in stallions and geldings.

* The curb chain should have been turned clockwise until it is flat and should lie in the chin groove, i.e. on a level with the mouthpiece of the bit. The last link of the chain should be hooked onto the right-hand curb hook in such a way that the chain remains flat throughout its length. If there is a link left over, it

should hang down outside the left hook. If there is more than one spare link, the links should be divided equally between both sides, or, if there is an odd number, there should be one more on the left than on the right.

Correct

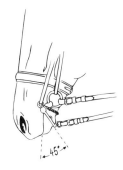

Correctly adjusted curb bit and curb chain. When a contact is taken on the rein, there is sufficient play for the cheek of the bit to form an angle of 45° with the mouth.

Incorrect

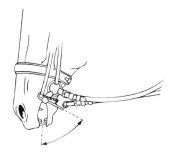

Too much play: curb chain too long, so that the cheeks 'bottom out'.

Incorrect

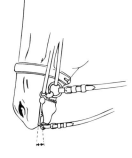

Not enough play: curb chain too short, so that the cheeks 'bind'.

The curb chain should be adjusted so that it comes into contact with the chin groove (i.e. its action begins to be felt) when the cheeks of the bit form an angle of forty-five degrees with the horse's mouth. If they will not go as far back as this, i.e. there is insufficient play, this means that the curb chain is too tight. The bit is then said to be 'binding'. If the curb chain is too long, the cheeks are able to come too far back, i.e. there is too much play and they 'bottom out'. Instead of being on the bars, the action of the bit is then on the corners of the mouth, which is incorrect.

A rubber or leather **curb guard** underneath the curb chain is a good idea for sensitive horses.

Putting the saddle on

Before the saddle is put on the horse, the stirrups irons should have been run up the back of the leathers and the girth have been attached to the girth tabs on the off-side and laid across the saddle. The saddle is then lifted onto the back near the withers and slid back into position

with the lie of the hair.

Special attention should be paid to the correct position of the saddle. Depending on the circumstances, on the material it is made of, and on its design, the numnah can be attached to the saddle either before or after it is put on the horse. It is important that there are no wrinkles underneath the saddle and that the numnah is well pulled up into the front arch of the saddle and does not work its way down and press on the horse's withers when the girth is tightened later and the rider's weight in the saddle.

After placing the saddle in the correct position, the rider goes round to the right (off) side of the horse, lifts down the girth and checks that it is lying flat and the right way round underneath the saddle flap. Next the girth is fastened, loosely at first, on the left (near) side of the horse. If the saddle is in the correct position, the girth will lie about a 10cm behind the point of the horse's elbow. Not until the saddle has been in place for a few minutes on the horse's back should the girth be tightened further.

Position of the saddle.

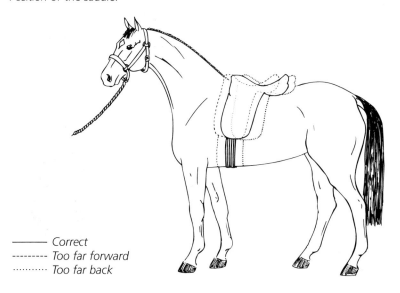

——— *Correct*
--------- *Too far forward*
·········· *Too far back*

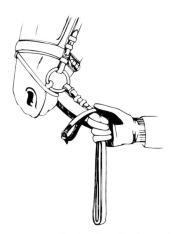

Holding the reins for leading the horse in hand.

Leading the horse in hand

If the horse is to be led with the saddle on, the stirrup irons should be run up the leathers and the leathers passed through the irons to prevent them slipping down. Dangling stirrups can frighten the horse, bang against its elbows or get caught on door fittings.

Horses are generally led from the left side. To lead the horse, take the reins over the head and hold them in the right hand about 10cm behind the bit rings. The reins should be separated in the hand by the index and middle fingers, with the right rein slightly shorter than the left. The ends of the reins are folded back through the palm of the hand and secured with the thumb.

If the horse is to be ridden in side-reins or a German standing martingale, these should not be fastened until the horse is in the school. When the horse is being led, side-reins should be clipped back onto the 'D's on the front of the saddle. In the case of a running martingale, the reins should not be threaded through the rings until the horse is ready to be ridden.

Special care should be taken when leading several horses one behind the other. There should be about two horses' lengths between the horses (about 5m). The instructor should keep stressing this. If the horse is to be led only a short distance, for example from the school to a nearby stable, the reins can be left on the horse's neck. However, this only applies in enclosed areas or buildings – anywhere else the reins must always be taken over the head.

If the horse is wearing a double bridle, the bridoon reins should be taken over the head and the curb reins left on the neck. For short distances it may be acceptable to leave both sets of reins on the neck in which case only the bridoon reins should be used to lead the horse.

When leading in hand, including for the

Turning the horse

purpose of parading or 'running up' a horse, all turns should be made to the right. There is then less chance of the horse overtaking the handler and of running into him if it shies. To turn the horse, the left hand should be raised and gentle pressure applied on the right rein. When dealing with a frightened horse the handler should avoid letting the reins get too long and should steady the horse by raising his left hand and speaking in a reassuring voice.

2 The Basic Training of the Rider

2.1 Planning the Training

Once the rider is used to the horse and to handling it, the ridden training can begin. The first stage consists in training the seat on the lunge. Under the supervision of the instructor, the rider must first acquire and practise a feel for sitting in balance and without tension in the three basic gaits. On the lunge he can do this without having to worry about steering and controlling the horse. Training the seat is relatively time-consuming, but it is well worthwhile because it makes the rider more secure and also enables him to make more rapid progress in the next stages of his training.

A general-purpose saddle should be used for the rider's basic training because it is suitable for training the rider in both the basic (or dressage) seat and the light seat. The use of specialised saddles is unnecessary in the early stages.

After a few lessons, when the rider has learned the basic principles of the seat and the application of the aids, he and other riders of similar standard can be put into small groups of about six to eight riders each. Each group should have an experienced rider at the front, since this makes it easier to teach the commands and school figures. It can sometimes be beneficial to allow the better riders in the group to swop horses temporarily so that they can gain more experience in riding the more difficult horses.

The instructor should ride the school horses occasionally so that he can get to know their individual characteristics and also so that he can correct their way of going if necessary. Suitable horses must be available both for the initial stages and the later stages of training.

NOTE A trained horse is the best teacher.

In a class lesson the student should ride with stirrups until he feels secure and confident. He can then, and only then, be asked to ride for part of the lesson with his feet out of the stirrups and the stirrups crossed in front of the saddle. The use of side-reins is recommended until such time as the rider is able, through correct use of the aids, to ride the horse 'on the contact'.

Demonstrations by experienced riders on advanced horses, with explanations by the instructor, and group visits to horse shows, stimulate the novice rider's interest and increase his general understanding and motivation.

For children, vaulting lessons are a very good way of getting the potential rider used to horses at an early age. The use of suitable ponies also makes life a lot easier for young riders in the early stages. Vaulting groups and ponies should be a feature of every riding school. (Vaulting and vaulting training are dealt with in Volume 3 of this series.)

The advice and explanations in the pages which follow are equally applicable to ponies.

Once the rider is secure enough in the saddle when riding in the school, training in the light seat, preliminary jumping lessons and riding out can be introduced.

An all-round basic training and plenty of variety in the lessons are the best and surest way to develop the rider's skill as well as his enjoyment of riding.

2.2 The Seat and Position

Mounting and dismounting

When riding in a school or outdoor arena, every rider must get used to positioning his horse on the centre line or in the centre of a 20m circle in order to mount, and must ensure that it stands quietly until he is on its back and ready to move off.

The reins should be buckled and lying on the horse's neck. The rider should always have one arm through the reins while he is preparing to mount, i.e. when pulling the stirrups down, adjusting the stirrup leathers or tightening the girth. It is irresponsible to leave a horse standing loose: even the quietest, best mannered horse can take fright and run away, causing serious injury to itself as well as to other horses and riders.

Stirrups should be adjusted before mounting. The length should be roughly equal to the length of the outstretched arm, with the fingertip on the tongue of the buckle by the stirrup bar. The length is about right if, with the leather taut, the stirrup reaches the armpit.

To mount, stand on the left (near) side of the horse, normally with your back to the horse's head, and proceed as follows:

* Hold the reins in your left hand on top of the horse's neck, with the left rein between the third finger and the little finger, and the right rein running through the palm of the hand. Both reins should be in light contact with the horse's mouth with a slightly stronger contact on the right rein if the horse fidgets.

* Step far enough back and to the right to be able to put your left foot in the stirrup.

* Grasp the mane in your left hand, and with your right hand take hold of the stirrup leather and turn it towards you.

* Place your left foot in the stirrup so that the stirrup is behind the ball of the foot, then lean your left knee against the saddle so that your toe does not disturb the horse.

* Stand on tip-toe on your right foot, catch hold of the cantle of the saddle with your right hand, hold on to the mane or the pommel with your left hand, transfer your weight onto your left foot, press your left knee against the saddle and push off energetically with your right foot, leaning your upper body forward as you do so.

* Placing your right hand on the pommel for support, swing your right leg slowly over the croup and lower your seat carefully into the saddle.

* Place your right foot in the stirrup and take up your reins.

A mounting block or stool can be used as an aid. This is of particular benefit to older riders and it also helps to prevent damage to the horse's back.

Mounting

Before moving off, the rider should transfer the right rein into his right hand and then make the horse stand still for a while before moving off.

If the horse is wearing a double bridle, the little finger separates the curb reins, with the left bridoon rein running through the palm of the hand and under the little finger, and the right bridoon rein between the index finger and the middle finger. All four reins are secured by the thumb on top of the index finger.

The **girth** should not be **tightened** immediately. It should be tightened while the horse is walking since this helps to prevent tension, and also prevents wrinkles being trapped under the girth. To tighten the girth, take the reins in one hand and

Tightening the girth.

lift your leg up in front of the knee roll on the side you intend to tighten it. With your foot still in the stirrup, use your free hand to tighten the girth one buckle at a time.

The horse must also be made to stand correctly for **dismounting.** The procedure is as follows:

* With the reins held correctly in the left hand, rest this hand on the top of the horse's neck and place your right hand on the pommel.

* Take your right foot out of the stirrup and swing it carefully over the horse's croup.

* You can then either:

    a) lower yourself down onto your right foot, with your left knee still against the saddle, then take your left foot out of the saddle and place it next to the right; or

    b) place both hands on the saddle to support yourself, take your left foot out of the stirrup and slide gently to the ground.

Both stirrups should then be run up the

bottom leathers and the girth slackened by a few holes. Again, while dismounting and afterwards, you must never let go of the horse: you should always have one arm through the reins so that you have some control if the horse takes fright.

The rider's seat

A correct seat forms the basis for the effective application of the aids. The rider must first find his balance on the horse. Only if the rider's seat is supple and free can he 'go with' the horse's movements without 'gripping up' or stiffening.

> **NOTE**   A balanced, free, supple seat is essential for the correct application of the aids.

There are three types of seat or position:
* the dressage seat (basic seat)
* the light seat (jumping/cross-country seat, forward seat)
* the racing seat (jockey seat).

> **NOTE**   With each type of seat, the amount of weight placed in the saddle can vary depending on the situation.

Basically, in the dressage seat, the weight is placed mainly on the horse's back, while in the light and racing seats it is taken off it. Between these two extremes of 'on' and 'off' there is, within each category, an infinite range of variations for use in different situations.

Lengthy and systematic training is required for the rider to be able to harmonise exactly, in whichever seat he is using, with the pace and the changes in the horse's centre of gravity. In both the dressage seat and the light seat, exercises play an important part in developing the necessary balance and fitness.

The dressage seat

The dressage seat, also known as the basic seat, forms the basis for all other types of seat. Careful attention should be paid to it when teaching the beginner.

The dressage seat, or dressage position, is used for the training of horse and rider on the flat, i.e. dressage-type work. It is also used with shortened stirrups in preparatory work for jumping and cross-country riding.

The dressage position can vary slightly depending on the build of the rider and the height and width of the horse. The rider should sit upright in the saddle so that a straight line can be drawn through his ear, shoulder, hip and ankle joint (which can be abbreviated to: shoulder, hip, heel).

The **seat** should rest in the lowest point of the saddle. The weight of the body should be distributed equally over the two halves of the seat and the inside thigh muscles. The muscles should be free from tension: any tension in the seat or thigh muscles will cause the rider to lever himself out of the deepest point of the saddle and sit 'above the horse'.

If the rider's seat is supple and free from tension (this quality is known as *Losgelassenheit* or looseness), the **thighs** can turn inwards slightly so that the knees rest flat against the saddle. The thighs should be as near to vertical as is possible without pulling the seat bones off the saddle. This will ensure the deep knee position which is so important for a deep seat and correct lower leg position, and for the correct application of the leg aids.

Turning the thigh outwards or too far inwards causes tension and prevents the rider from sitting deep in the saddle.

The **knee** should be slightly bent so that the foot, seen from the side, is underneath the rider's centre of gravity. Correctly adjusted stirrups will help to maintain this bend.

A 'fork seat' may result if the stirrups

The dressage seat

are too long. The legs have to stretch too far, so that the rider's weight is taken on the thighs more than on the seat and he can no longer push effectively with his lower legs.

Riding constantly with stirrups which are too short can result in a 'chair seat' and can also lead to the rider not sitting deeply enough in the saddle. Moreover, if the lower legs are positioned too far forward the rider will not be able to use them correctly.

The **lower legs** should slope backwards from the knee (the angle depends on the length of the leg), with the inside of the calf maintaining a soft contact with the horse's body. This means that the lower leg will lie just behind the girth, completing the perpendicular line through the shoulder, hip and heel.

The **feet** should rest in a natural position on the stirrup tread, almost parallel to the horse's sides and with the tread just behind the widest part of the foot. In movement the ankle should flex, causing the heel to sink slightly so that it becomes the lowest point of the rider's body. Tense, inward-turned toes are a fault, as are toes turned outwards or heels pressed down to an exaggerated degree.

The **upper body** should be erect and the rider should be seated in the centre of the saddle with his body free from tension. He should avoid 'collapsing' one hip, which would prevent him from being correctly in balance. His spine should therefore be exactly above the centre of the saddle, and should retain its natural 'double 'S' ' shape. A convex, 'banana-shaped' back or a concave 'hollow' back causes stiffness and prevents the rider from applying the aids effectively.

The rider should sit **tall** but not in a forced, tense way. The muscles of the upper body should be sufficiently taut to keep the rider in a steady position but should not be so tight that they prevent the body from going with the movement of the horse. This entails the **pelvis** following, or accompanying, the movements of the horse's back. We say that the rider 'accompanies the horse with his seat', and by 'seat' we mean here the combination of his pelvis, hip-joints and thighs. Only if he has a sufficiently deep and supple seat can the rider be in harmony with the horse's movements.

The allowing and supporting of this elastic movement of the seat by the muscles of the upper body is described as 'bracing the back'* or 'tightening the back muscles', although for the purposes of following the movement (rather than, for example, riding a half-halt) the muscles are only moderately tightened. This tightening and allowing action (i.e. constantly varying the tone) of the muscles of the trunk takes place more or less automatically.

The **head** should be carried freely and erect with the rider looking ahead over the horse's ears. Sticking the chin out or pulling it in excessively detract from the suppleness of the upper body and so from the rider's ability to accompany the horse's movements with his seat.

The **shoulders** should be carried naturally and without tension, and should

---

*The German expression, literally translated, is 'bracing the small of the back', which is not strictly correct from a physiological point of view, because Man does not have muscles dedicated to controlling the small of the back. However, this is an accepted expression in the context of classical equitation and has come to refer to the tightening and relaxing of the muscles of the trunk (abdominal muscles and deep muscles of the lower back) and the resulting rocking movement of the pelvis (see also pages 52 and 59).

be drawn back just sufficiently to give the chest a slightly convex appearance. The upper arms should hang down freely from the shoulders, just in front of the vertical. The **forearms** and the **elbows** should be lightly touching the body. Clamping the arms against the body often causes the shoulders to be drawn up and leads to stiffness in the hands. Sticking the elbows out ('chicken arms') detracts from the suppleness of the seat and the independence of the rein aids.

The **hands** should be closed but not clenched. They should be held with the knuckles vertical since this is the only position which allows the rein aids to be conveyed subtly enough from the wrist to the horse's mouth. The thumb should be slightly bent and rest on the top of the reins to prevent them slipping through the hands.

> **NOTE**   Only a supple, balanced seat allows the rider to apply the leg and rein aids independently of the movements of his upper body. It is an essential prerequisite for the effective application of the aids.

Forearm, rein and bit should always be in a straight line when viewed both from above and from the side. Only if this line is unbroken can the rider give correct, sensitive rein aids and maintain a soft contact with the horse's mouth.

The light seat

The light seat has a wide range of applications. It enables the rider to take the weight off the horse's back, for example, when riding over fences, when riding out and when riding young horses. Depending on where it is used and how forward it is, it is given different names, for example, the cross-country seat and the jumping seat.

A jumping or general-purpose saddle is the right shape and has the necessary forward-positioned knee-rolls to enable the rider to ride correctly in the light seat. The stirrups are considerably shorter in the light seat than in the dressage seat. The actual length varies and depends on the individual situation. For a moderately light seat, two or three holes may be enough, whereas in the more extreme form, where

The light seat

the horse's back is completely relieved of weight (e.g. for show-jumping and cross-country) they need to be shortened by as many as four or five holes.

> **NOTE**   Using the light seat enables the rider to adjust particularly well to changes in balance and pace. He should also be able to make smooth transitions between the different forms of the light seat.

To adopt the light seat the rider bends his upper body forward from the hips – the actual angle depends on the circumstances. The weight is taken more on the thighs, knees and heels. In the more moderate form of the light seat, the seat should remain as **close to the saddle** as possible since this makes the rider's balance more secure. At fast paces and when jumping, where more of the weight is taken off the horse's back, the seat should be more **out of the saddle.**

In the light seat, just as in the dressage seat, the rider must be supple in his **pelvis, hip joints and thighs.** Stiffness or

Variations of the light seat: the amount of weight in the saddle varies but the principle remains the same.

too much movement in the upper body are faults and they interfere with the balance of both horse and rider.

In the light seat, the knee is more bent on account of the shorter stirrups. The rider remains firm in the saddle by keeping his **knees closed** firmly against it.

The **lower legs** are positioned next to the girth. The flat side of the calf is in contact with the horse's body and is used to give the driving aids. Allowing the lower leg to slip back has an adverse effect on the rider's balance. In jumping, this fault often results in the rider returning to the upright position too early so as not to tip forward, thus disturbing the horse in its back.

The foot is pushed slightly further into the stirrup, so that the widest part is on the tread. The foot must always remain underneath the centre of gravity to ensure that the rider is balanced at all times.

The **heel** should be the lowest point of the rider's body. The ankles should be flexible and slightly bent, thus providing a steady, springy support, and also enabling the lower legs to remain steady. If the heels are drawn up, the rider cannot absorb the movement properly, the lower legs slide back, and the rider gets in front of the movement.

> **NOTE**   A firm knee position, a constant lower leg position, and downward flexing heels form the basis of the light seat.

The forward position of the **upper body** should be achieved by bending only at the hips. The spine should retain its natural shape; a convex or hollow back must be avoided.

The **upper arms** should be carried forward slightly so that the **elbows** are slightly ahead of the body. The position of

Moderate version of the light seat

the **forearms** should be such that as far as possible a straight line can be drawn through the forearm and rein to the horse's mouth. In the light seat, as in the dressage seat, the rein and leg aids should be **independent** from the movements of the rider's body.

The **hands,** with the knuckles vertical, are held one on each side of the horse's neck. The length of the reins depends on how forward the seat is.

The **head** is held erect and carried freely with the rider looking forwards.

For **jumping,** the rider needs to be particularly well balanced so that he can accompany the horse's movements in the different phases of the jump and adapt his position accordingly. Attention should be paid to the following:

• During the **take-off** phase the rider should remain folded forward from the hips, in the light seat. At the same time he should press down sufficiently into his

Light seat over a jump

The individual phases of the jump

Approach: the approach is ridden in a rhythm and at the basic canter pace used for jumping.

Take-off: the rider goes smoothly with the horse's movement. The hands go forward in the direction of the horse's mouth.

heels to keep his lower leg beside the girth and prevent it sliding back. For higher fences the rider will need to fold forward more on take-off.

While keeping his seat, knee and heel low, the rider must yield sufficiently in the direction of the horse's mouth to allow the necessary stretching of the neck. There should still be a light contact with the mouth.

* **In the air** over the jump, the body should be inclined further forward, which will result in a greater clearance between the seat and the saddle. The degree will depend on the height of the jump and the arching of the horse's back. What is important is that the rider goes smoothly with the horse and remains in balance.

* During the **landing** phase the upper body should adjust smoothly to the change in the position of the horse's centre of gravity. The rider should avoid tipping forward or getting behind the movement. Straightening up too soon

disturbs the horse in its back and can lead to incorrect use of the hindquarters ('hindquarter faults').

Before, during and after the jump, the knee and lower leg should remain as steady and firm as possible. Throughout the jump the hand should keep a steady, elastic contact with the horse's mouth. The head should be held erect, in particular so that the rider can see the next fence when he lands.

Looking back at the fence is bad practice and disturbs the concentration of both horse and rider.

The racing seat

The racing seat is used by experienced riders for galloping and is only required during the 'steeplechase' phase of a three-day event. In the racing seat, none of the rider's weight is in the saddle.

Because of the short stirrups, a racing saddle or a particularly forward-cut general-purpose saddle is necessary. In the racing seat the stirrups should be a few holes shorter than in the light seat so as to

In the air: the weight is off the horse's back. The knees, lower legs and heels do not move from their position.

Landing: the upper body comes back.

lift the rider's seat clear of the saddle. The rider's weight is taken mainly on the knees and heels.

Firmly closed knees and a **perpendicular lower leg** position are required for the rider to be able to maintain his balance at speed. The rider absorbs the horse's movement by allowing his **heel** to flex downwards from the ankle

in time with the stride.

The **upper body** should be folded forward almost parallel with the horse's neck.

The **upper arms** should be in front of the body. The hands should be positioned one on each side about 10cm below the top of the neck. The elbows should not stick out. The rider accompanies the head

The racing seat

and neck movement of the galloping horse by flexing elastically at the elbows while still maintaining a constant, steady contact with the horse's mouth. The horse's nose should be well in front of the vertical. The reins can also be used as a **bridge** on the horse's neck to prevent the rider disturbing the horse and to enable him to stay in balance at all times (see page 64).

Rising and sitting trot

Rising trot is one of the first basic exercises in the rider's training and is taught as part of the early lunge lessons. It lessens the effect of the rider's weight on the horse's back and enables even a beginner to go with the movement almost without disturbing the horse. It is less tiring for the rider than sitting trot.

In rising trot, instead of sitting in the saddle for each step, the rider rises at one step (using his knee and stirrup to support him) and then sits softly back down again at the next.

When **rising,** the seat is 'pushed' out of the saddle by the horse's action and impulsion. It is wrong for the rider to actively pull himself out of the saddle, since this detracts from the fluency of the horse's movement and interferes with the action of its back.

For the rider to be able to rise and sit elastically, his **feet** must be directly

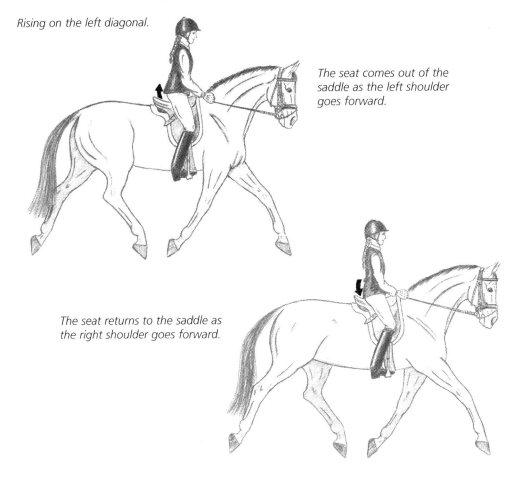

Rising on the left diagonal.

The seat comes out of the saddle as the left shoulder goes forward.

The seat returns to the saddle as the right shoulder goes forward.

underneath his centre of gravity. The **knee** must therefore stay bent. The **heels** must remain the lowest point of the rider's body.

The rider's **lower legs** should remain steadily in position, in contact with but not clinging to, the horse's body so that they can push in time with the stride. As the rider sits elastically down, he gives a slightly stronger aid with his weight and legs to stimulate the hind feet to step well forward. In so doing he is exercising a positive influence on the paces and helping to make the horse more supple and 'through' *(Durchlässigkeit)*.

The **upper body** should remain upright and the rider should sit down in the centre of the saddle. Leaning very slightly forward when rising is better for maintaining the fluency of the trot than rising stiffly. When riding with **short stirrups** in particular, leaning forward slightly from the hips enables the rider to be more in harmony with the horse's movements and the changes in balance. However, he must avoid tipping forward, pushing his seat out behind, losing the contact with the horse's mouth or turning his legs and feet outwards with stiff knees and ankles.

The rider rises as one diagonal pair of legs swings forward (e.g. the right hind foot and the left forefoot) and sits down elastically as the other diagonal pair moves forward. The diagonal takes its name from the forefoot, so the rider is said to be trotting on the right diagonal when he rises at the same time that the right forefoot is picked up, and on the left diagonal when he rises in time with the left forefoot. In Germany, the rider is said to be trotting 'on the left or right hind leg', i.e. if he is trotting on the right diagonal, he is said to be trotting on the (diagonally opposite) left hind leg.

When riding in the school, the rider always trots on the outside diagonal, i.e.

he rises in time with the inside hind leg, because this leg is better able to support the rider's weight, especially on turns and circles. The rider can tell when the inside hind foot is stepping forward, because the outside shoulder moves forward at the same time. Because in the trot the legs move in diagonal pairs, sitting down as the horse's outside shoulder comes back brings extra weight to bear on the inside hind leg.

When changing the rein, the rider changes the diagonal by sitting down for two steps, or more to start with (although it must be an even number), before rising again.

When out on a ride, the diagonal should be changed at intervals so that each pair of legs does the same amount of work. The rider must make a conscious effort to do this since most horses have a tendency to 'manoeuvre' the rider onto one diagonal, most often the right.

It usually takes a certain amount of practice for the novice rider to acquire the deep, supple seat required for **sitting** to the horse's movement, especially at the trot and canter. Exercises on the lunge, including riding without stirrups, are particularly beneficial in this respect.

For the **seat** (i.e. the combination of his **pelvis, hip joints and thighs**) to be able to **move elastically with the horse's movements** and for the position in the saddle to be deep and supple, the rider must first be able to sit with a natural, easy posture, with the muscles of his trunk elastically taut, and be able to follow the horse's movements correctly with his pelvis.

These movements of the pelvis are achieved by constantly adjusting the tension, i.e. the degree of tone, of the different muscles of the trunk. This is also known as 'moderately bracing the back'

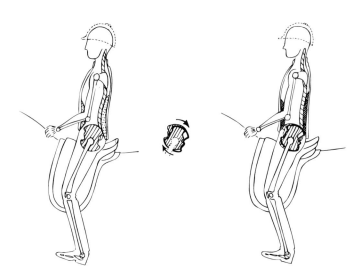

When sitting to the movement, i.e. sitting trot and canter, the rider makes almost imperceptible rocking movements with his pelvis. This involves the synchronised tightening and relaxing of the various muscles of the trunk (i.e. 'the back muscles').

(see Section 2.2 The Dressage Seat). If the muscles are correctly in tension and in balance as a whole, the rider 'allows' this process to happen as part of the natural balancing process rather than actively making it happen through muscular effort.

When the horse moves, its back moves up and down. At the point when the back comes up slightly, if the rider has a supple seat which is free from tension, his back muscles will tighten slightly, i.e. he will 'brace his back' moderately (the small of the back becomes flat rather than slightly concave). In other words, the abdominal muscles and the deep muscles of the lower back contract, causing the pelvis to tilt so that it slopes forwards from top to bottom.

In the next phase of the movement, when the horse's back goes down slightly, the muscles are allowed to lengthen (while keeping a certain tone, i.e. remaining taut): the small of the rider's back is allowed to become slightly concave and the bottom of the pelvis moves backwards slightly again.

Hence the rider makes almost imperceptible rocking movements with his pelvis and seat in order to keep his seat 'glued' to the saddle. Without this synchronised contraction and relaxation (varying the tone or tension) of the muscles of the trunk, the rider would either be too limp or too stiff and would not be able to sit in harmony with the horse's movements.

If the rider possesses sufficient 'looseness' and elasticity, accompanying the horse's movements in this way will be a more or less **automatic** process. This moving 'with' the horse should never be exaggerated: it should be in proportion to the amount of movement.

In walk and canter in particular, accompanying the movement with the seat and pelvis is often misunderstood and exaggerated. As a result, the rider sits **against the movement** of the horse. This can prevent the horse using its back properly and lead to loss of rhythm.

Training the seat

Basic principles and aims

Instruction in the basic or dressage seat forms the basis for all rider training. The novice rider should be taught balance, looseness, a feeling for rhythm, enjoyment of the harmony of movement and security. Guided by his instructor, he should be given the time and opportunity to learn and become thoroughly familiar with these basic prerequisites.

> **NOTE**   Only if he has a balanced, supple seat will the rider's aids be correct. Only correctly, consciously applied aids result in the rider acquiring the correct 'feel' and enable him to act upon the horse predictably and consistently. Even experienced riders should never stop working on the basic principles of the correct seat.

Relevant gymnastic training can be used both as preparation and as part of the education of beginners and experienced riders alike. However, as well as the rider's age, posture problems must also be taken into account. More emphasis should be placed on loosening up and stretching than on developing strength.

Appropriate exercises should be used immediately before as well as during the ridden instruction. The rider, as well as the horse, needs to develop 'looseness' *(Losgelassenheit).* A true horseman will only ask athletic feats of his horse if he has his own body under control.

Prerequisites for training the rider

The use of suitable horses is essential for seat and position training.

For lunge work, as well as for other forms of rider training, it is essential to have quiet horses which are established in their way of going. Only if the horse will work through its back (wearing side-reins if necessary) and is comfortable to sit on can the novice rider learn to sit correctly and the more advanced rider correct his faults.

In the early stages, training the seat can be done with or without the saddle. Sitting directly on the horse's back allows the rider to feel the horse's movements better. It is a good idea to use a roller (e.g. a vaulting roller) so that the rider has something to hold onto.

A general-purpose saddle is the most suitable for seat and position training with a saddle and for all other basic training. It is especially good for teaching the rider to make smooth transitions from the basic seat to the light seat and back again.

For **seat training on the lunge** the horse should be fitted with side-reins. Exercises can be performed with or without stirrups. For work without stirrups, the stirrups are best removed from the saddle completely.

Seat training and gymnastic exercises should not be performed for too long at a time. Exercises should be done first in walk then in trot and at a slow canter.

Training in the dressage seat

* The beginner rider should start by sitting in a natural position (according to what feels right to him) at halt. Then he should simply turn his upper leg slightly inwards from the thigh so that his knee lies flat against the saddle without gripping it.

* He should sit down in the saddle or on the horse's back without tensing the muscles of his seat or inner thigh.

* The lower legs and feet should hang down in a relaxed manner.

* The rider should practise laying his lower leg against the horse's side from the hanging position. This exercise should be repeated again and again so that the rider learns to keep a correct, soft contact with the horse's body and does not 'cling' with his lower legs.

* Only after the previous steps have been followed should the upper body be positioned as required. It must be explained to the rider that when his chest is slightly convex as it should be, this causes the vertebrae of the back to be drawn forwards. He must therefore be taught from the outset to push his lumbar vertebrae back slightly in order to avoid having a hollow back.

* To teach the rider the correct position of the lower legs, arms, hands and head at the halt, the instructor can 'guide' the body into position with the horse halted.

At this stage of the training it is important not to overdo things, otherwise there is a danger that the rider will suffer muscle cramps and will lose confidence. It is a good idea to use one horse for two or three riders, since this allows them to have breaks in between riding and also to do exercises off the horse.

The first canter lessons should also be on the lunge. The rider can use his hands to steady himself and also to help him to sit deep in the saddle. The inside hand should hold the pommel, and the outside hand the cantle. The rider should feel that he can absorb the horse's movement in his seat (pelvis, hip joints and thighs). The canter can be practised either with or without stirrups, at the instructor's discretion, depending on the rider's ability and the circumstances.

Training in the light seat

The light seat must be taught just as systematically as the dressage seat. In order to prevent setbacks attention must be paid to the following:

* The instructor should realise that different muscle groups are used in the light seat and in the dressage seat. Apart from being taught the principles, the rider should also therefore receive organised gymnastic and fitness training.

* The stirrups should be shortened gradually by three to five holes. The basic principles of the light seat can be taught first at halt or in walk. However, it is easier to get the feel of adjusting to the movement, to changes in the balance, and to the pace, when the horse is moving, and especially in trot and canter. The transition from the basic seat to the light seat can be practised in trot.

* Moving smoothly backwards and forwards through the whole range of seat positions must be practised in order to develop the rider's suppleness at an early stage.

* The rider needs to re-learn his balance in the light seat and in its different variations. He can use a neck strap to steady himself to start with and to hold onto in times of need.

* The rider can first practise moving his hands forward in the direction of the horse's mouth while walking and trotting over cavalletti. Special attention must be

paid to the position of the knee, lower leg and heel (the foundation of the seat).

* Once the rider's has a firm enough seat, the light seat can be practised over natural, unlevel terrain and up and down slopes.

Firmness and balance can be further developed through exercises (including without reins or without stirrups).

Alternating between rising and sitting trot develops the rider's suppleness and looseness, as does working with the weight alternately in and then out of the saddle.

Grids can be used to help the rider to develop an independent seat, i.e. to make his seat independent of his hands and vice versa. Grids can also be ridden without reins, i.e. with the reins knotted on the horse's neck. The horses used must obviously be quiet and reliable.

Seat and position problems

Even with systematic training it is still possible to get seat and position problems. It is important to correct any faults promptly. Once they have become established they are extremely difficult to eradicate, and so all instructors and riders should be aware of these faults and their consequences so that corrective action can be taken straight away. This action should not consist simply in correcting individual position faults: rather, the connection between the rider's position and the way the horse moves should form the basis for all corrections.

Causes
Problems in the way the rider sits can have various causes, e.g.
* wrong teaching or bad habits
* posture problems coupled with poor

body awareness
* lack of feel for the rhythm of the movement
* inadequate, badly fitting saddle
* poor corrective action by the instructor.

Many seat and position faults result from stiffness, i.e. lack of looseness. Special attention should be paid to developing this quality during the basic training, although experienced riders also need to keep working at it.

Poor physique and bad posture (e.g. a hollow back, heavily muscled thighs, a hunched back or weak abdominal muscles) can sometimes be improved, or even cured completely, through appropriate exercises.

Before starting to correct the rider, it is essential to check the saddle. Saddles which have lost their shape as a result of long use and misuse, so that the deepest point is no longer in the centre, are not suitable for the rider to learn on. They also put additional strain on the horse's back.

Seat problems do not usually occur singly. One fault tends to lead to another – for example:
* knees drawn up/heels drawn up
* stiff shoulders/unsteady hands
* lack of flexibility in the seat and hip joints/nodding head
* head to one side/weight wrongly distributed.

Apart from generalised tension, and the resulting unsteadiness and insecurity, the most commonly occurring problems are the 'chair seat' and the 'fork seat'.

In the **chair seat** the seat is pushed out of the deepest point and towards the cantle of the saddle. The seat muscles are tightened in a misguided attempt to 'brace the back'. This also causes the thighs and knees to be drawn up so that the rider can no longer use them properly. This fault is usually the result of too short stirrups or of riding all the time in a jumping saddle or in a saddle in which the deepest point is too far to the rear.

The consequences of the chair seat are:

* The rider is no longer sitting on his seat bones.

* There is a reduction in the size, and therefore the effectiveness, of the area in contact with the saddle.

* There can be very little movement in the loin region, and so the rider's ability to 'go with' the rhythm and the movement is impaired.

* The rider sits in a hunched position with his chest hollowed.

* The head becomes unsteady and is pushed forward instead of being carried erect.

Common position faults in the dressage seat.

* The lower leg comes too far forward as a result of the incorrect position of the knee and thigh. It is then impossible to give the leg aids correctly.

* The rider can no longer use his hands independently of the rest of his body, and so he 'hangs on' the reins.

Correcting the chair seat

The rider needs to learn to sit with his seat further forward in the deepest part of the saddle. The thighs, knees and ankles need to be relaxed downwards. Training on the lunge on a comfortable horse can be useful. The rider needs to 'grow tall', i.e. stretch his whole body so that he adopts a more extended position. It helps to bear in mind the desired perpendicular through shoulder, hip and heel.

In the **fork seat** there is too much weight on the thighs and groin. The weight comes off the seat bones and the lower legs slide back. Often the back is

Chair seat

Fork seat

hollowed. This fault is often caused by riding with stirrups which are too long or by a saddle in which the deepest point is too far forward.

The consequences of the fork seat are:

* It does not provide the basis for a balanced seat.

* The seat bones and the muscles of the seat are neither in contact with the horse nor deep in the saddle. This makes it impossible to use the weight aids effectively.

* Because the back is hollowed, the loins lack the flexibility to 'go with' the movement. The seat becomes stiff and bangs against the saddle in canter.

* The rider cannot use the driving aids properly.

* The rider's hands are no longer independent. They are either pushed stiffly downwards or the rider places them on the withers for support.

Correcting the fork seat

The rider needs to transfer his weight from his thighs to his seat. Shortening the stirrups slightly can be helpful. Basically, the rider must learn to sit in the deepest part of the saddle. Exercises involving bending the upper body forward can also be beneficial.

Problems in the light seat

The commonest faults in the light seat and in jumping are failing to keep up with the movement or getting ahead of it. Both are caused by lack of **balance** and inability to adapt the balance to the changes in the centre of gravity.

Some causes of getting **in front of the movement** are:
* allowing the lower legs to slip back
* drawing the heels up
* seat too far above the saddle
* dropping the contact with the horse's mouth just before the jump
* losing the rhythm on the approach.

Some causes of getting **behind the movement** are:
* lower legs too far forward
* having too much weight in the saddle before the jump
* hands acting in a backward direction
* lack of elasticity in the seat (pelvis/hip joint/thigh combination).

The light seat must become so well established that the rider can use it for schooling and suppling the horse, and can keep the horse consistently 'in front of the leg' while riding in this position. It is a mistake to think that exaggerated 'sitting in' (whilst still in the light seat) will encourage the horse to make a greater effort and go forwards more. There is often too much weight in the saddle in between jumps. If the rider is elastically 'going with' the rhythm of the horse's movement, he will be able to do the pushing with his lower legs. A firm 'base' (knee, calf and heel) is therefore of the utmost importance since without this the upper body position cannot be correct.

Stirrups which are **too long** make it more difficult to balance. They cause the rider to get in front of or behind the movement, depending on the situation. They also encourage him to put too much weight in the saddle, i.e. not to take the weight off the horse's back sufficiently.

Common position faults in jumping.

'In front of the movement'

'Behind the movement'

Stirrups which are too short do not allow a steady position of the knee; the rider is too high above the horse and will tend to get behind the movement.

Standing up in the stirrups, often with straightened knees, is wrong and needs to be corrected. It prevents the rider going smoothly with the movement, especially before and over the jump.

Practising the correct seat on the lunge, riding across natural, unlevel terrain, cavalletti work, gymnastic jumping and dedicated gymnastic exercises are some good ways to improve the light seat.

2.3 The Application of the Aids

The rider influences the horse through his **weight,** his **legs** and the **reins.** His actions are called aids. The leg and weight aids have by their nature a predominantly forward-driving effect, whereas the rein aids have more of a restraining action.

The aids are **coordinated,** i.e. combined, to obtain the desired gait, pace and position, and to provide overall control of the horse. They should be subtle and discreet. This is both the aim and the criterion by which they are judged. As training progresses, the aids should become progressively less visible to the onlooker and progressively more meaningful to the horse.

All aids are combined actions of weight, legs and reins. These actions are not successful when used singly: correct application of the aids entails delicate coordination of all the aids.

It is important to realise that man's natural reaction, when trying to achieve something or to prevent it happening, is to use his hands. In riding, however, the aim is to increase the effectiveness of the weight and leg aids so that the rein aids can be made progressively more subtle.

NOTE   The driving aids are more important than the restraining aids.

The intensity of the aids depends on the horse's sensitivity, its stage of training and on what the rider is trying to achieve. The aids should always be applied gently to start with, and the intensity increased or decreased as required. If strong aids are necessary, the rider should always return to lighter aids afterwards so as to preserve the horse's sensitivity and not make it increasingly 'dead' to the aids.

Insensitive aids spoil the horse, whereas frequent praise makes for a better working relationship between rider and horse. Caressing or patting the horse, or using the voice (discreetly and unobtrusively) also help to relax the horse and so to improve its looseness (Losgelassenheit).

> **NOTE**   As the training progresses, the aids will become progressively more subtle and unobtrusive, until finally the horse responds to aids which are almost imperceptible to the onlooker.

The weight aids

The weight aids are essentially forward-driving aids, although they also back up the (ever more finely coordinated) leg and rein aids.

The rider can use his weight in the following ways:
* by increasing the weight on both seat bones
* by increasing the weight on one seat bone
* by easing the weight on the seat bones.

The stiller and more supple the rider's seat, the better the horse will respond to these aids.

The rider must be able to ensure that his own centre of gravity coincides with

that of the horse in any situation. He is then light and comfortable for the horse to carry. The difficulty lies in adjusting to the horse's constantly changing balance, i.e. its dynamic centre of gravity.

A rider who is not sitting in balance, and cannot move with the horse, will disturb the horse's rhythm and carriage and restrict its freedom of movement.

Increasing the weight on both seat bones is used to increase the activity of the hind legs, e.g. in all halts and half-halts, and in all transitions. In conjunction with the forward-driving leg aids, this weight aid stimulates both hind feet to step further forwards in the direction of the centre of gravity and to push off more energetically.

Increasing the weight on both seat bones, or on one seat bone, is done with the upper body in a natural, erect position (though it helps for the rider's back to be moderately 'braced' (see page 44) so that he can accompany the horse's movements).

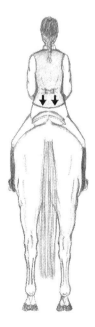

Increasing the weight on both seat bones.

Increasing the weight on the seat bones entails **bracing the back** more strongly: this means that the rider, while contracting and relaxing the muscles to allow his seat to accompany the movement, momentarily exaggerates the phase where the abdominal and lower back muscles are tightened. This action is repeated if necessary for several steps or strides. The effect is to encourage the horse to step further under its body in the direction of the centre of gravity and to take more weight on its hind legs.

Tightening the back muscles in this way should never be a continuous action. Incorrectly contracting the muscles of the trunk dulls the horse's responses and blocks the forward movement rather than making the horse engage more. It also prevents the rider's pelvis moving with the horse's movement with the result that the seat becomes fixed and stiff. When performed correctly, the action of increasing the weight on the seat bones is almost imperceptible to the onlooker.

Without these short-acting, relatively intensive weight aids, exercises such as half-halts, which serve to prepare the horse for the transitions and the different movements, would rely too much on the rein aids. There would be nothing to tell the hind feet to engage more in the direction of the centre of gravity and carry more weight.

When using these weight aids it is absolutely essential for the rider to ensure that he is always in balance with the horse. Leaning back, stiffly tensing the seat muscles and drawing up the knee and thigh (with the lower leg sliding forwards) prevent this aid from being used effectively and are incorrect.

> **NOTE** If the rider is in a position to tighten his back muscles when necessary, i.e. to 'brace his back', he will be able to influence his horse correctly. (See also page 44.)

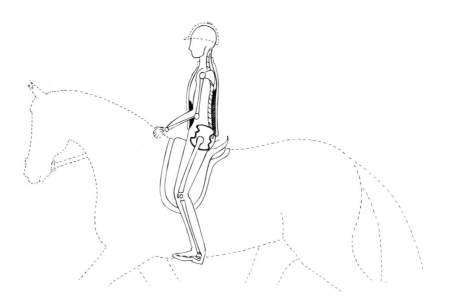

'Tightening the back muscles' ('bracing the back') involves a momentary tightening of the muscles of the abdomen and lower back.

Incorrect

Correct

Rider collapsing the hip – the weight falls out onto the wrong side.

Putting more weight on one seat bone.

Increasing the weight on one seat bone is an important back-up to the rein and leg aids in all movements where the horse is flexed or bent, and in well-schooled horses it is the most important aid. The rider places more of his weight on one seat bone than the other. This causes a slight lowering of the hip, and of the knee, which remains bent. The rider should place more weight on the stirrup on the same side.

To a well-schooled horse this weight aid is a signal to turn and thus bring its balance back in line with that of the rider.

The rider **eases the weight on the seat bones** when he needs to ease the weight on the horse's hindquarters or back when schooling on the flat, e.g. when riding young horses, when loosening the horse up and in the early stages of teaching the horse the rein-back.

The rider places a little more of his weight onto his thighs and stirrups. His seat remains in the saddle, while his upper body comes forward slightly in front of the vertical depending on how much weight is to be taken off the seat bones.

When using weight aids on **bends** and **curved tracks** the rider must be completely in balance and with the movement, whether he is using the dressage seat or the light seat. His hips and shoulders should remain in their natural position; the inside shoulder and hip should not be 'left behind'. Pushing the horse forwards excessively is incorrect.

If the rider has a fundamentally correct, supple seat, and applies the aids clearly and deliberately but at the same time sensitively, he will continue to sit in balance when the horse turns.

The leg aids

The leg aids are used as a signal to the horse to start moving and as a means of keeping the movement going. Hence leg aids always have a driving or pushing action. They can be used in the following ways:

* forward-driving leg aid
* forwards-sideways pushing leg aid
* regulating leg aid or 'guarding' leg.

The **forward-driving leg aid** is applied just behind the girth so that the heel is vertically below the hip. If the lower legs are softly in contact with the horse's body, they will have the effect of increasing the alternating sideways curving movement of the horse's body which occurs naturally in

time with the stride. As the horse's body bulges outwards, the leg is pushed sideways and the weight of the leg causes a slight pressure to be felt on the horse's side.

This means that the horse feels the action of the leg at every step or stride, and keeps itself going without the rider having to use his legs actively. Obviously, though, the effectiveness of this action depends on the horse having acquired, through its basic training, the required level of responsiveness.

Briefly tightening the calf muscles

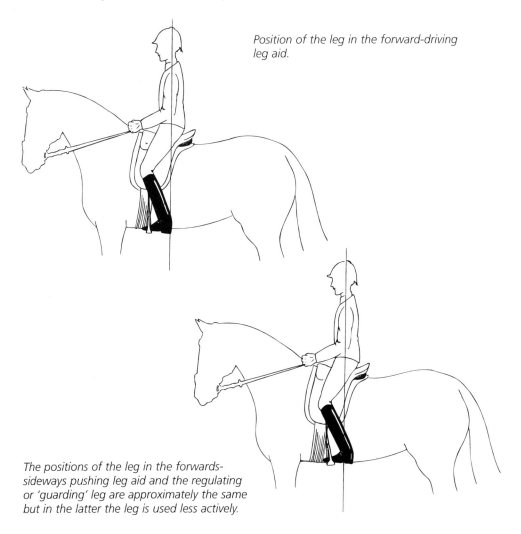

Position of the leg in the forward-driving leg aid.

The positions of the leg in the forwards-sideways pushing leg aid and the regulating or 'guarding' leg are approximately the same but in the latter the leg is used less actively.

emphasises the signal to the horse to push off with its foot from the ground. This aid is used especially to coincide with the lifting of the hind foot on the same side.

With horses which do not respond to an aid of such short duration, the rider needs to make the horse more responsive by using stronger aids at first. On no account should his legs remain clamped to the horse's sides.

The **forwards-sideways pushing leg aid** causes the horse to step forwards and sideways with the hind leg on the side the aid is applied, or the hind leg and diagonally opposite foreleg, depending on the exercise. The rider's leg should be about 10cm further back than its normal position. It must never be drawn upwards. Like the forward-driving leg, this aid is most effective when used just as the hind foot is being picked up.

The position of the **regulating** or **'guarding' leg** is approximately the same as that of the forwards-sideways driving leg but it is used less actively than the latter. While **one** leg is giving forward or forwards-sideways pushing aids, the other must act in a regulating or 'guarding' capacity on the opposite side. Only if the aids work together in this way will the action of sideways pushing leg achieve the desired effect.

The purpose of the regulating or 'guarding' leg is to limit the sideways movement of the hindquarters or to stop them evading sideways. Hence it keeps the hind feet following in the same track as the forefeet, so that the horse works equally onto the contact on both sides. The regulating leg is also partly responsible for the forward movement.

As a basic rule all the aids are applied with the leg quietly against the horse. Stronger aids should be used only on a short-term basis and in individual cases.

They should then be used sharply, as a 'warning'.

The rein aids

Holding the reins

When riding with a snaffle bridle the reins should be of equal length and untwisted and should pass between the third finger and the little finger with the smooth side of the leather facing outwards. The ends of the reins should pass out of the hand over the second joint of the index finger and hang down, buckled together, inside the off (right) rein and on the off-side of the horse.

The fingers should be closed. The thumbs should be slightly bent and lightly pressed down on top of the rein where it passes over the index finger, to prevent it slipping. The hands should be held with the knuckles vertical and at such a height that the forearm, the hand and the horse's mouth are approximately in a straight line. The distance between the hands depends on the thickness of the horse's neck – the line from the elbow to the horse's mouth also needs to be straight when seen from above.

Adjusting the reins

When adjusting, i.e. shortening the reins, the rider takes hold of the rein to be

Correct

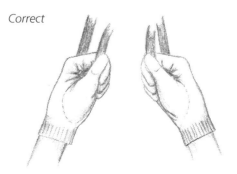

Holding the reins.

shortened with the fingers of the opposite hand, opens the hand holding the rein, and slides it down the rein as required. Often, the rein needs to be shortened only slightly, for example, to make the reins the same length or to maintain the contact with the horse's mouth.

Scrambling down the rein with the hand, without securing it with the opposite hand, is incorrect practice. It upsets the horse in its mouth and disturbs the contact. Moreover, it is impossible to adjust the length of the rein accurately in this way.

When riding turns and circular tracks, the outside hand should always remain as close as possible to the horse's neck or withers so that the whole length of the rein is in contact with the horse's neck.

Raising one hand a bit higher than the other for a moment is sometimes practised by advanced riders as a correction. On turns and circular tracks only the inside hand should be used in this way.

In some situations, for example riding up and down slopes or when riding for long periods in the light seat, the rider can use the technique known as **bridging the reins** to give him extra help in keeping his balance. In a bridge, the spare end of the left rein, after it comes out through the top of the left hand, passes down through the palm of the right hand so that the two hands are connected by a section of rein about 15-20cm long. This bridge is positioned on top of the horse's neck in

Incorrect

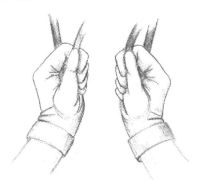

Stiff wrists

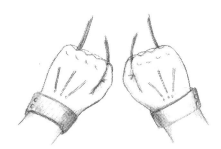

Hands facing downwards

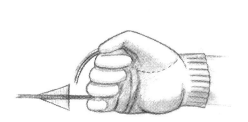

Fingers not closed on the reins

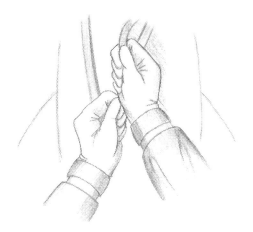

Hand crossing the horse's neck

front of the withers, with the thumbs securing the ends on each side of the neck. Hence the thumbs form pivots which help the rider to keep an even contact with the horse's mouth.

Incorrect hand positions include:

* **Stiff wrists,** which prevent the rider having an elastic contact with the horse's mouth.

* **Fingers not closed on the reins,** with the third finger pulled forward, which allows the reins to become longer and longer and encourages the rider to bring his hands back towards his stomach.

* **Hands facing downwards,** so that the rider cannot give sensitive rein aids from his wrist. Instead, he will tend to use his whole arm or his body so that the action of the rein is wrong, especially when using an 'asking' rein aid.

* **Crossing the rein over the horse's neck** is a serious fault because it makes the action of the bit in the horse's mouth incorrect. As a result, the horse's neck is constricted so that it tilts its head from the poll.

The **rein aids** must be used in accordance with the principles of correct training. The following points are therefore particularly important:

* rein aids should only be given in conjunction with leg and weight aids

* only if the horse is letting the aids through and working through its back can the action of the rein aids pass through the mouth, poll, neck and back and reach the hindquarters.

The rein aids can have the following actions:
* yielding
* asking
* non-yielding
* regulating or 'guarding'
* sideways-acting or 'opening' rein.

Yielding and asking rein aids must always be considered as a pair. Which comes first, the yielding or the asking, depends on the situation and the position and carriage of the horse. What is important is that the aids are finely tuned and sensitively given from the wrist. This is only possible if the hand is held correctly, with the knuckles vertical, and if the wrist is supple.

Yielding and asking rein aids are always used in conjunction with the appropriate weight and leg aids. They are used, for example:
* in all half-halts, and so in transitions from one gait to another or within a gait (increasing and decreasing the strides)
* in halts
* to improve the self-carriage and the horse's contact with the bit
* when about to begin an exercise
* when flexing or bending the horse
* as necessary in the rein-back.

Depending on the intensity, the **asking rein aid** consists in either closing the fingers momentarily, or for a stronger effect, turning the hand inwards slightly from the wrist. The hand must **never** remain fixed in position. If the horse does not respond immediately, this aid must never be allowed to degenerate into 'pulling on the reins'. Instead the hand should yield, and further asking/yielding aids should be given as required.

If the **yielding aid** follows an asking

aid, it consists in returning the hand to the basic position. However, the rider may start with his hand in the basic position, then open his fingers slightly or move his hand forward a little without first giving an 'asking' aid. Care must be taken to yield the rein smoothly and not in a jerky movement so that it 'springs loose'. There should always remain an elastic contact between the hand and the horse's mouth. Hence the hand should become lighter in its action, rather than dropping the contact.

In certain situations, yielding from the wrist is not enough and the elbow and shoulder also need to be involved. One example is when the horse needs to be allowed to lengthen its neck (e.g. when 'lengthening the outline' in extended paces and 'taking the rein down'). The action of the yielding rein must always be forwards in the direction of the horse's mouth.

> **NOTE**   Every asking rein aid must be followed by a yielding aid.

The **non-yielding rein aid** is used when the horse goes against or above the contact. Applied with the appropriate lightness and finesse, and used on a horse which 'lets the aids through' correctly, it can also be used instead of the asking rein.

To give this aid, the hands close tightly, without altering their position, until the horse yields to the bit and becomes light in the hand. However, the hands should not act in a backward direction or continue their action for too long. This aid must be used in conjunction with bracing the back and with forward-driving leg aids.

It is important that the hand becomes light again in its action as soon as the horse becomes light in the hand and yields through the poll. On turns and circular tracks this applies especially to the inside hand.

Whenever the horse is required to be bent or flexed, the **regulating rein aid or guarding rein** complements the action of the inside asking rein aid, the purpose of which is to obtain the flexion.

To use a regulating rein aid, the rider yields with his outside rein just enough to allow the amount of flexion at the poll, or bend in the neck, which has been asked for by the inside rein. However, this rein aid also serves to prevent excessive bend in the neck and 'falling out' onto the outside shoulder. With this aid, as with the others, the hand needs to be kept low.

If the horse does not respect this aid sufficiently, it may be necessary to increase its responsiveness by a brief 'asking and giving' action on this rein.

The **sideways-acting rein aid or opening rein** is used especially in turns, to indicate the direction to the horse. This aid is especially useful on young horses and when teaching the lateral movements. The side asking rein aid is used at the same time to flex the horse or to bend it in preparation for a turn. The rider first turns his hand in slightly from the wrist to obtain the flexion or bend then he carries it a few centimetres away from the neck, as if to lead the horse's nose in the required direction. However, at the finish or before repeating it, this movement must be followed by a marked yielding action in the direction of the horse's mouth. An example of a possible use of this aid is to begin the turn on the haunches.

The hand, in conjunction with the driving aids, determines the 'frame' within which the horse should move. The rein aids should never be used just as a means of making the horse yield at the poll (to 'bring the head down').

> **NOTE**   Many riders tend to use the rein aids too strongly, i.e. to make too much use of their hands and not enough use of their legs and seat. This tendency must be strongly discouraged.

The horse is said to be **'on the bit'** when it is working happily on the contact, and is accepting the rein aids, and there is a steady, soft connection between the rider's hand and the horse's mouth both at the halt and in movement.

The horse is described as **'on a long rein'** when the head and neck are carried naturally but with the horse keeping a constant contact with the rider's hand. The rider, for his part, keeps just enough contact for the horse to bend slightly at the poll.

The horse is said to be **'on a loose**

'On the bit'

On a long rein

On a loose rein

rein' when there is no longer any contact between the rider's hand and the horse's mouth. The reins are held at the buckle.

Riding with a double bridle

The horse must be ridden in a double bridle only if the following criteria can be met: the horse must be established in its contact and acceptance of the bit and supple enough to 'let the aids through'. Only then will the more refined aids, which result from the use of the curb bit, be effective. All movements and exercises should be practised in a snaffle before they are ridden in a double bridle in competitions.

> **NOTE**   The most important prerequisite for riding with a double bridle is a correct, balanced, supple seat which allows the rider to use his hands independently.

Before using a double bridle, the rider needs to learn to use the reins with more finesse. The rein aids are given in the same way as when using a snaffle bridle, but the elasticity of the hands is even more important since the lever action of the bit increases the intensity of its action on the mouth. The rider needs to be constantly on his guard against unintentionally putting too much pressure on the curb reins.

In turns, the rider must be especially careful to yield the outside curb-rein since otherwise the horse will tend to tilt its head from the poll.

> **NOTE**   When riding in a double bridle, the rider should check the length of his reins especially carefully and frequently.

There are different ways of holding the reins when riding with a double bridle. Usually, the reins are held **in both hands** (i.e. two reins in each hand, or '2:2'), and with the bridoon rein underneath the third finger, like the snaffle rein, and the curb rein between the middle and third fingers. Both reins then pass over the top of the index finger, where they are secured by the thumb, and the ends of the reins hang down on the off (right) side. In the salute, the rider takes the two right reins in his left hand. The ends of both sets of reins hang down underneath the right reins by the side of the horse's neck.

In another method of holding the reins in both hands, the bridoon rein is held underneath the little finger, with the curb rein between the little finger and the third finger. The action is similar to that of the previous method.

In yet another method, the bridoon rein is held underneath the third finger, with the curb rein under the little finger. This method in particular should only be used by experienced riders, because when the hand is turned inwards the action of the curb rein predominates.

Holding three reins in one hand and one in the other ('3:1'), **holding all the reins in one hand** and the **Fillis method** (snaffle reins over the forefingers and curb reins under the little fingers) are only recommended for advanced riders and then in special cases.

Special considerations for using the aids in the light seat

The same principles apply to the use of the aids in the light seat as in the dressage

The most commonly used methods of holding the reins in two hands when riding with a double bridle.

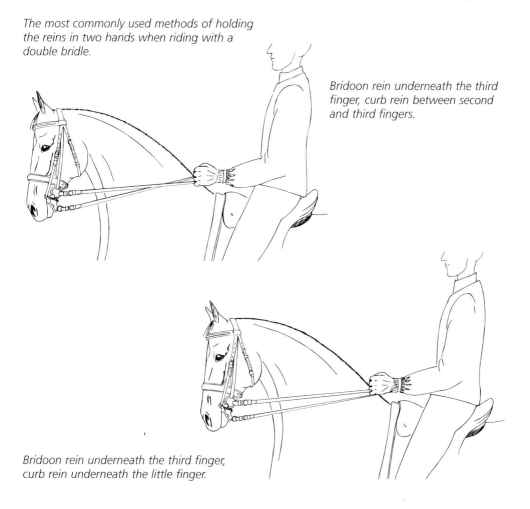

Bridoon rein underneath the third finger, curb rein between second and third fingers.

Bridoon rein underneath the third finger, curb rein underneath the little finger.

seat. Even though the rider's weight is not directly on the horse's back, it is still effective as an aid. The horse must always remain in front of the driving aids (in front of the leg).

To **slow the pace** or **shorten the strides,** for example, between jumps, the rider moves his weight back by straightening his upper body slightly. His seat comes closer to the saddle. This action stimulates the horse to spring further forward with its hind legs in the direction of its centre of gravity and to place more of its weight on its hindquarters. This can be important particularly in turns, and sometimes before a jump, as well as when riding transitions from one gait to another and within a gait.

When **increasing the pace or the strides,** the lower legs send the horse forward, increasing the energy and the forward thrust from the hindquarters. The faster the pace, the further the upper body is inclined forward, taking more of the weight off the horse's back.

People often make the mistake of 'sitting in' and driving the horse with their seat. This is unnecessary if the horse is correctly 'on the aids'. It can even put the horse off its stride and make it hollow its back. Only if the horse is not stepping far enough forward under its centre of gravity should the rider use his weight in this way to increase the activity of the horse's hindquarters before asking it to increase its strides. However, the upper body should never be allowed to come behind the vertical.

In **turns** and on **circular tracks** the regulating ('guarding') leg and the outside rein are particularly important – especially at faster paces, the horse is inclined to fall out onto the outside shoulder. In the light seat too, the horse should be contained or 'framed' by the rider's aids and should

remain supple and 'through'.

As in the dressage seat, the rein aids should be independent of the movements of the rider's body and the contact between hand and mouth should be just as steady and elastic. Because in the light seat the weight in the saddle varies, and with it the 'forwardness' of the rider's position, the reins need to be adjusted more frequently.

When ridden in the light seat, and especially for jumping and riding across country, the horse still needs to be **'on the contact',** although not necessarily 'on the bit' in the dressage sense. A galloping horse, ridden in the forward seat, has a more forward centre of gravity and also needs to use its head and neck like a balancing pole. It is therefore wrong to 'place' the horse's head (mainly by use of the hands) as is so often seen in the show-jumping arena. Moreover, this also restricts the horse's field of vision and upsets its balance.

Special considerations for using the aids in the racing seat

In the racing seat, the **forward-driving** effect is produced by the natural movement of the rider's upper body (in time with the gallop) acting through his knees. On bends, the rider needs to move his weight towards the inside and increase the contact on the outside rein to keep rider and horse in balance with each other.

As a rule, racing **fences** should be **jumped** in the same rhythm and the rider should not lean backwards to 'counterbalance' the forward movement. Training should be aimed at getting the horse to jump fluently and to judge by itself when to take off. When allowing and 'going with' the stretching of the horse's neck over the jump, the rider should still keep a steady contact with the mouth. He should also remain as still as possible so as not to disturb the horse.

Auxiliary aids

The rider's **voice,** the **whip** and the **spurs** are used to make the rider's intentions clearer to the horse and to reinforce the weight, leg and rein aids.

Use of the **voice** is indispensable in the early training of young horses. It should be used sparingly with older horses or they tend either to become dependent on it or to cease to respond to it. In dressage competitions, audible use of the voice is not permitted.

The tone is the most important factor in the use of the voice. A calm, low-pitched voice has a soothing effect, whereas a word or a short, sharp click of the tongue at exactly the right moment is an effective way of giving the horse extra encouragement.

A reassuring voice is helpful when teaching a new exercise (such as the halt or rein-back) and also when the horse has been upset by outside influences.

Stimulating the horse with the voice can serve to make it more alert, to reinforce the leg aids and to make the horse concentrate on the rider. Thanks to its large, mobile ears, the horse has far better hearing than man, and loud words are not only unnecessary but also can upset it.

If several riders are using the school at the same time, voice aids should be used discreetly and kept to a minimum.

> **NOTE** The primary role of the voice is to give the horse confidence.

The **whip** is used to make the horse more alert. In flatwork (dressage) it is also used to increase the activity of the hind legs.

The **dressage whip** is held a little way in from the end, near to its centre of gravity. It should lie obliquely across the rider's thigh, pointing from front to back. The rider should use the whip to touch the horse just behind his lower leg, taking care not to disturb it in its mouth. Using the whip in the flank area or behind the saddle is not usually practical, since in many cases it not only fails to make the horse work more actively with its hind legs but it also causes it to raise its croup. The dressage whip can also be used to touch the horse on the shoulder in order to reinforce the regulating or sideways-pushing aids.

Use of the whip is beneficial in the following cases:

* on very green horses to support the forward-driving action of the weight and legs
* on more experienced horses which are not responsive enough to the leg.

In an indoor school the whip is usually carried on the inside to prevent it touching the wall, otherwise it should be carried on the side it needs to be used.

If the whip needs to be changed over into the other hand, the rider puts both reins in the same hand as the whip and pulls the whip slowly upwards out of this hand with the free hand. The hand holding the whip then returns to its normal position and takes the rein back from the other hand.

It takes great tact and sensitivity to judge when, how and how hard to use the whip. A short, sharp tap is more effective than constant 'niggling', which only serves to deaden the horse's responses. The horse should respect the whip but not fear it. The rider should never hit the horse through impatience. The whip, like the leg, should be used in time with the movement. Use of the whip which disturbs the horse's rhythm is always incorrect.

For jumping, a special **jumping whip** is used. It is about 75cm long and should have a thick, comfortable handpiece and a leather 'keeper' at the end.

It is used, as necessary, on the horse's shoulder, in time with the movement if possible. The noise made by the leather 'keeper' serves to reinforce the rider's driving aids. It can also be used to support the outside rein and prevent the horse falling out onto its shoulder.

When using the jumping whip to correct a disobedience, the rider puts both reins in one hand for a moment and applies the whip behind his leg.

Spurs are used first and foremost to enable the rider to apply his leg aids with more finesse and, secondly, to reinforce the leg aids. In this secondary role their use can complement that of the whip. Before using spurs the rider must have learned to use his legs in a controlled fashion and independently of his seat. As a general rule, blunt spurs 2-3cm long are sufficient during basic training.

As with all the aids, the use of spurs should be kept 'brief and to the point'. Constant 'niggling' only serves to dull the horse's responses.

If the horse lacks impulsion, or respect for the driving aids, and has to be sent energetically forwards with the whip or spurs, the rider must take the utmost care not to disturb its mouth with his hands while doing so.

Using auxiliary reins and martingales

Different types of side-reins and martingales can be used to help the rider

who is not yet confirmed in the use of the aids. Their use allows him to concentrate on his seat and to practise applying the aids.

> **NOTE**   When using auxiliary reins and martingales in schooling, the aim must always be to make them superfluous eventually.

The type of rein or martingale used and its adjustment depend on the shape of the horse and how it reacts to the aids (see also p.28). However, it must always be long enough to allow the nose to be carried in front of the vertical or vertically: it must never pull the nose behind the vertical. Side-reins, of which there are several different types, can be used when training the rider's seat (on and off the lunge) and for schooling on the flat. For slow hacking (walking and trotting), side-reins are sometimes used as a safety measure. They must be removed for riding over cavalletti and rough or sloping ground. Of the martingales, only the running variety should be used for jumping.

When using the most commonly found types of auxiliary reins or martingales, the following principles apply.

Ordinary (single) **side-reins** place the horse on a contact, with a slight flexion at the poll, making it easier for the rider to get the horse to respond to his aids. The side-reins should be attached to the girth on each side in such a way that they cannot slip down. The ideal height is about 10cm above the point of the horse's shoulder. The side-reins are attached at the other end to the snaffle rings. They should be adjusted so that they are equal in length and so that the head is carried in the required position with the neck slightly bent at the poll. They should never be so short that the nose is behind the vertical.

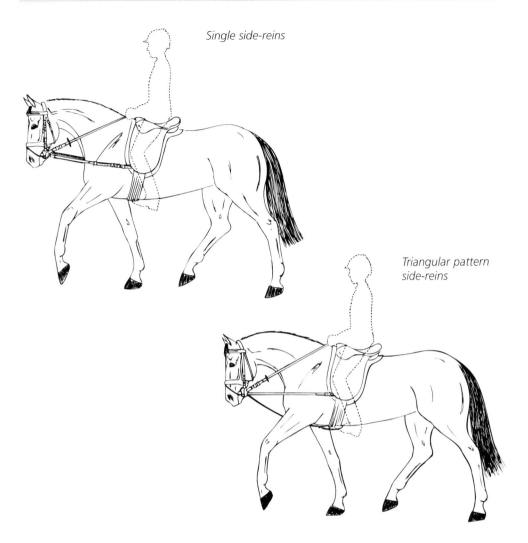

Single side-reins

Triangular pattern side-reins

They should be put on after the girth has been done up. Side-reins should always be undone when walking for long periods, and at the end of the lesson and for jumping.

The same principles apply to **triangular pattern side-reins** as to single side-reins. Triangular pattern reins have the advantage that they allow the horse to stretch forwards and downwards when required. They also allow the novice rider to feel more easily when the horse is trying to lean on the bit. This is a sign that he should increase his driving aids in order to make his intentions clearer to the horse.

Because the horse cannot establish a steady, elastic contact when this type of side-rein is fitted, using it on its own for lungeing is not recommended. Ordinary side-reins and running reins (double side-reins) are more suitable.

The action of the **running martingale** is only felt in certain circumstances. For example, if the horse tries to evade the action of the bit by raising its head excessively, a correctly adjusted running martingale will make it more difficult for it to do so. Also, the action of the bit is

Running martingale

transferred from the lips to the bars of the mouth, making the action of the rider's hand on the mouth softer. Moreover, the neckstrap of the martingale can provide extra support for the rider when riding up slopes or jumping.

When the neckstrap has been passed over the horse's head, the martingale is attached to the girth between the forelegs. The reins are unbuckled, each rein is threaded through the appropriate ring, then they are buckled together again on top of the horse's neck.

With the running martingale correctly adjusted, when the horse's head is carried normally, the rein forms a straight, unbroken line from the rider's hand to the horse's mouth. Like the standing martingale, if the running martingale is too short, its action has a negative effect in that it causes the horse to resist the constant downward pressure and in so-doing to develop the muscles on the underside of the neck.

Other types of auxiliary reins are draw reins, the Chambon and the Gogue, which should not be used in basic training. These types of rein should only be used by experienced riders since their action is complex. Inappropriate use can do lasting damage to the horse's training and confidence and can sometimes cause injury.

2.4 'Feel'

One of the most important things for a rider is 'feel', also known in literature as 'equestrian tact'.

The rider needs 'feel' in order to be able to apply the aids:
* in the correct manner
* at the right moment
* in the right intensity
* to apply the weight, leg and rein aids in the correct ratios.

It is essential that the rider learns and develops 'feel' in order to be able to gradually **refine his use of the aids.**

The **horse's response** shows whether the aid has been correctly applied, and enables the rider to check the correctness and effectiveness of his aids. He needs to learn to distinguish between right and wrong and to adjust his reactions accordingly.

'Feel' is reflected in the rider's way of training young horses as well as in his handling of more advanced horses.

The rider:

* is able to detect possible faults in their early stages and so avert them or nip them in the bud

* keeps out of trouble by reverting to an easier exercise if the horse shows signs of rebellion

* feels immediately when the horse yields or resists and so is able to react accordingly

* can distinguish between high spirits and disobedience

* can tell the difference between a horse which is tired and one which has been overfaced or pushed too hard.

> **NOTE** 'Feel' is essential for a harmonious, confident and effective relationship between rider and horse.

There are various natural talents and qualities which make it easier to learn and develop 'feel'. Certain qualities which are simply normal human characteristics are an advantage, if combined with a love and respect for horses. These qualities are, for example:
* sensitivity
* adaptability
* agility
* quick reactions

* ability to concentrate
* a feeling for rhythm and movement.

Equestrian tact or 'feel' can be developed and refined by various methods: on a ready-trained, supple horse, through meaningful explanations (by an instructor) or through practice and trying things out. The best way is to use a combination of all three methods.

2.5 The Co-ordination and Effect of the Aids

The rider's aids should serve as signals to the horse that it should move in a certain way and so perform certain exercises.

The rider influences the horse through a combination of weight, leg and rein aids. Any one of these aids used on its own cannot be effective. Only if these aids are correctly coordinated can they work properly.

The correct coordination of the aids is only possible if the rider has a correct, supple seat, 'looseness' (Losgelassenheit) and 'feel'. The rider must be fully in control of his body if he is to be in a position at all times to apply the aids independently of the horse's movement and in the correct balance and intensity.

Successful use of the aids depends on the skill, coordination and finesse with which they are applied and not on the amount of strength used. Hence a rider with no great physical strength is sometimes considerably more effective than his stronger counterpart.

The synchronisation of the driving and restraining aids is crucial to the horse's way of going and its obedience. The alternating use of these aids, precisely synchronised with the rhythm of the movement, is essential if a correct and lasting effect is to be achieved.

If the driving aids are insufficient and the action of the hands is too strong, the horse cannot step forward far enough under the centre of gravity. The rider must always endeavour to ride his horse forwards with impulsion, even in the collected paces.

NOTE In the combined, co-ordinated use of the driving and restraining aids, the driving aids must always predominate.

3 BASIC EXERCISES

3.1 Riding-in and Exercises to Obtain Looseness (Losgelassenheit)

Only if the horse is mentally and physically free from tension can it produce its top performance and achieve its full potential. Hence looseness (Losgelassenheit) needs to come before all else. The rider needs to be made aware of this connection in his early training.

Riding and all other work with the horse, i.e. lungeing or loose jumping, should begin with a **riding-in** or **'loosening'** phase. Loosening prepares and warms up (increases the blood supply to) the horse's muscles, tendons and ligaments. The joints do not develop full mobility until they have been in movement for a while and the synovial fluid has worked into the layers of cartilage. Inadequate working-in can result in injury, such as pulled or torn muscles and damage to the joints.

Only correct loosening exercises will result in the horse swinging through its back and lengthening and stretching its frame when required. These exercises must be tailored to suit the horse and aimed at getting the muscles to contract and extend without tension, i.e. at enabling them to work with maximum efficiency.

The riding-in period also serves to loosen up the rider, especially if he has been under strain at work or sitting down for long periods. Dissolving mental tension and focusing the minds of horse and rider on the session ahead are the best preparation for a harmonious workout.

As a general rule the horse should be ridden for **at least 10 minutes in walk** on a loose or long rein. Then trot work can begin, starting with rising trot.

The horse should be worked with a light contact, in a forward-going, rhythmic trot, on straight lines and gentle curves (outside track and circles). It should work with increasing 'looseness'. Riding the horse forward does not mean pushing it out of a rhythm (hurrying), which can cause tension. If the pace is too slow, the trot will lack spring so that there will be no encouragement for the hind legs to step further forward. This can prevent the horse going forward onto the contact sufficiently or working correctly through its back.

Once the initial stiffness has worked off, canter work can be introduced. The horse should be ridden in a forward-going rhythmical canter on a circle or on the outside track. Frequent transitions between trot and canter are especially good for reducing tension in the back and will result in the horse giving the rider a more comfortable ride and responding better to the aids.

Depending on the stage of training of rider and horse, the following exercises can be used for loosening the horse and riding it in:

* walk on a loose or long rein, then:
* rising trot on large diameter curved tracks

* canter work on large diameter curved tracks, possibly using the forward seat
* transitions from trot to canter and canter to trot
* leg-yielding, turns on the forehand
* changing the rein out of the circle
* single shallow serpentine loops, and serpentines across the whole width of the school (3-4 loops)
* lengthening the trot and canter strides.

> **NOTE** There is no fixed sequence of exercises: the order varies from one horse to the next. The important thing is that, for each horse, the trainer or rider knows what exercises or movements, in what sequence, in what number, and perhaps also on which rein, will best achieve his aim of making the horse looser *(Losgelassenheit)* and more supple or 'through' *(Durchlässigkeit)*.

'Taking the rein forward and down' is practised frequently in the riding-in period, in between different exercises, as a means of testing and improving the activity of the horse's back. At the end of the riding-in period in particular, this exercise can be used to check that the horse can stretch sufficiently in all three gaits.

The **duration of the riding-in period** depends on the horse and its level of training. As a rule, 20-30 minutes, including 10 minutes in walk, is sufficient to obtain looseness *(Losgelassenheit)*. **lungeing, loose jumping or turning the horse loose in the school** can also be incorporated into the working-in process, provided that the period of walk at the beginning is not neglected.

Hacking out just before the schooling session is particularly good for working off mental tension.

Towards the end of the working-in phase, **cavalletti** can be introduced or small gymnastic jumps in the case of more experienced horses and riders. These are particularly good for encouraging the horse to swing through its back. However, the rider should take care not to ask for too much. Otherwise, usually, not only will he fail in his aim of loosening the horse but also he will simply be creating further tension.

Jumping and cross-country riding need to begin with a working-in period. Horse and rider also need to be sufficiently loosened up before going out hacking, hunting, etc. This is the only way to ensure that the aids will be applied correctly, and therefore that the horse will be under control, which is essential if injury to horse and rider are to be avoided.

In the **main phase** of the lesson, any tensions which arise should be dealt with through the use of loosening exercises. At the end of the lesson, in the **relaxation phase**, the rider should check again, particularly by asking it to 'take the rein forward and down', that the horse is truly loose *(Losgelassenheit)* and that there were no hidden tensions present during the lesson.

There should be frequent periods of **walk**, on a long or loose rein, throughout the lesson, to give horse and rider the necessary breaks.

With more advanced horses, additional exercises can be incorporated into the working-in period, for example:

* leg-yielding away from and back to the wall
* leg-yielding on the side of the circle which is not against the wall
* changing the rein within the circle
* figures of eight
* decreasing and increasing the circle.

With loosening exercises it is never a question of 'the more the better'. They should not drag on until the horse is tired. Correct, systematically performed loosening exercises put the horse in a better position to perform, and make it capable of a higher level of performance, as well as increasing its mental well-being.

> **NOTE** Experience shows that improving 'looseness' *(Losgelassenheit)* makes nervous horses become calmer and lazy horses become more active.

3.2 Basic Schooling Exercises and Dressage Movements

Bringing the horse onto the aids

Bringing the horse onto the aids entails pushing it forwards from behind onto the contact, i.e. into the hand, so that both at the halt and in movement, a steady but soft, elastic connection is established between the rider's hand and the horse's mouth.

This connection is known as 'contact'. It provides the rider with a constant, sure means to communicate his intentions to the horse at all times. The contact should always remain elastic, and even if it sometimes needs to be increased momentarily, it should never become 'dead' and unyielding. The horse's position while maintaining this contact will vary depending on its level of training, as well as on the gait and the amount of engagement. However, the nose should always remain in front of the vertical, or vertical at most, with the poll remaining the highest point. (Exceptions to this rule are taking the rein forward and down, and the long outline assumed by young horses.)

> **NOTE** A correctly schooled horse will readily accept both the driving and the restraining aids in all transitions and turns.

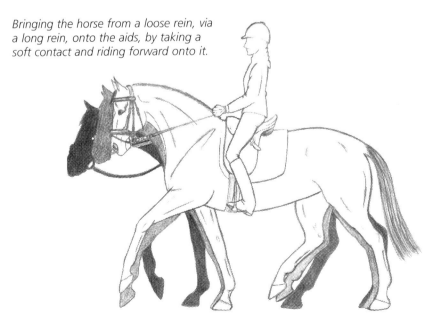

Bringing the horse from a loose rein, via a long rein, onto the aids, by taking a soft contact and riding forward onto it.

The horse is, as it were, 'framed' by the weight and leg aids, and the rein aids. What is most important is that it goes actively and freely forward – without hurrying – within this frame. This is only possible if the horse is 'loose' and therefore free from tension in its back, and if it 'gives' at the poll, and accepts and responds to the driving aids ('allows itself to be pushed'). It will then also be encouraged to relax in its mouth. Relieving the tension in the neck muscles allows the ducts of the parotid glands, behind the edge of the lower jaw, to open so that saliva is released. The movements of the mouth and the action of swallowing cause this saliva to appear as foam around the edges of the lips.

If the horse stiffens against the bit, the rider should increase and maintain the contact (non-yielding rein aid) to get the horse to 'give' in its poll. One way to do this is on a circle, with the horse flexed and slightly bent. Since the horse bends around the inside leg, it is particularly important for the outside rein and leg

to act in a regulating or 'guarding' capacity. The outside rein should 'allow' just the right amount of flexion, and the outside leg should prevent the hindquarters from swinging outwards. As soon as the horse yields, the inside hand must become light again.

The above is just one of many possible ways of putting the horse 'on the aids'. The skill lies in discovering the right exercises for the horse and rider concerned, and for the individual situation, while at the same time respecting the basic principle of riding the horse forwards from behind – 'from leg to hand'. The rider must never forcibly 'place' the head with his hands.

Taking the rein forward and down

Taking the rein forward and down, and giving away the reins (also called stroking the horse's neck) are ways of checking whether the horse is correctly on the aids.

Taking the rein forward and down.

Taking the rein forward and down is a test of rhythm, looseness *(Losgelassenheit)* and the correct contact. This exercise is an excellent way of increasing the horse's confidence in its contact with the bit and the rider's hand. At the same time it helps to develop the balance, especially in the case of young horses.

The reins are gradually lengthened as far as the horse is prepared to stretch to maintain the contact or until it is 'on a long rein'. The horse should stretch forwards and downwards onto the contact. The rider may have to increase his forward-driving aids in order to keep the hindquarters active.

The horse should stretch down at least until its mouth is level with its elbow but not so far that it loses its balance. The nose should remain vertical or in front of the vertical. During this exercise, the rider's hand should go forward slightly in the direction of the horse's mouth so that the reins can be shortened afterwards more easily and discreetly.

Taking the rein forward and down can be performed in any gait, preferably on a circle.

If the horse is working correctly, with 'looseness', it will remain in balance and will maintain the same rhythm and degree of collection. The rider will find himself increasing his driving aids.

If when the rider 'gives' the rein the horse does not stretch its neck forward or snatches the reins out of the hand, these are clear indications that there is still some tension in its neck and back muscles. Almost always, the rider has been using too much hand and not enough leg, resulting in an incorrect contact.

Frequent, short bouts of 'taking the rein forward' are more effective for strengthening the muscles than leaving the horse for **too long** in a stretched outline. The latter can also quite easily lead to the horse falling onto the forehand, which defeats the object of this suppling exercise.

The exercise can be ended at will by closing the fingers and shortening the reins again or it can end with the horse being given a loose rein.

Giving away the reins or stroking the horse's neck.

Giving away the reins or stroking the horse's neck serves to test the horse's self-carriage. It should show whether the horse is confirmed in its obedience to the weight and leg aids.

To give away the reins the rider pushes his hands forward approximately 10-20cm along the top of the horse's neck for a few strides and then returns them to their original position. The horse's nose may come slightly further forward in front of the vertical. The horse should remain in self-carriage and the pace and rhythm should stay the same.

Sometimes, the rider may choose to give away one rein only, usually the inside rein. This is a way of testing whether the horse is accepting the outside rein properly after the flexion or bend has been increased.

Riding the horse in different gaits

Within the three basic gaits of the riding horse – walk, trot and canter (for descriptions of the sequence of footfalls

and the different forms of each gait, see Section 4.3) – there are variations based on the degree of collection and so the length of the steps or strides. Particular importance should be attached in all gaits to the rhythm and regularity: the steps or strides should be equal both in length and duration.

Walk

The walk is a stepping movement in four-time with no moment of suspension. Different forms are the medium walk, the extended walk and the collected walk. Of these, only the medium walk is used in basic training. Extended and collected walk are more difficult exercises which are not required until a later stage of training (See Book 2, *Advanced Techniques of Riding*).

As well as a clearly defined four-time beat, the basic requirements in all forms of walk are activity, freedom and adequate length of stride (the prints of the hind feet should be in or in front of the prints of the forefeet, depending on the type of walk).

Medium walk

With the horse on the aids, to perform a forward transition from halt into walk, the rider sends the horse forward with his legs and weight, at the same time yielding with his hands but still maintaining a soft contact.

The rider keeps the walk active, forward and regular by elastically following the movement and keeping his legs lightly in contact with the horse's sides. He 'gives' sufficiently with his hands, and from his shoulders and elbows, to allow the slight nodding movement of the horse's head and neck.

Too strong use of the hands is one of the commonest faults when riding in walk and can seriously detract from the horse's rhythm and looseness. Pushing too hard, clamping the lower legs against the horse, and pushing alternately with the legs in an incorrect and exaggerated way can also lead to loss of rhythm and regularity due, for example, to the hind legs not stepping forward equally under the body. In Germany, the horse is then said to be 'going short/long' (one hind foot steps further forward than the other).

If the feet are moved forward and set down in lateral pairs, the horse is 'pacing' instead of walking. Pushing wrongly and rigid hands are the usual causes of a lateral-type walk, which is very difficult to correct.

Trot

The trot is a two-time movement with a moment of suspension. The different forms are the working trot, the medium trot, the collected trot and the extended trot. Of these, it is mostly the working trot, the medium trot, and sometimes the collected trot, which are used in basic training. 'Lengthening the strides' is an exercise used to prepare the horse for medium trot.

To perform a forward transition into trot, the aids are the same as for the transition into walk, only stronger. In trot the rider's seat (the combination of his pelvis, hips and thighs) should accompany the horse's movements. This is achieved

Working trot

through controlled tightening and relaxing of the back muscles (as described in Section 2.3). The seat and aids are used to monitor and maintain the rhythm and impulsion of the trot.

In **transitions** from one form of trot to another – increasing and decreasing the strides – the horse must accept the driving and the restraining aids, i.e. it must 'let the aids through' *(Durchlässigkeit)*. To increase the strides the rider prepares the horse with a half-halt, or several half-halts, and then uses his weight and both legs positively, simultaneously and smoothly to send the horse forward and make it cover more ground. At the same time the rider must 'give' sufficiently with his hands to allow the necessary stretching of the horse's neck and lengthening of the frame. The contact and self-carriage should not be affected.

Decreasing the strides is also preceded by one or more half-halts. It is important that the rider increases his driving aids during the half-halt(s) since otherwise the horse will fall onto the forehand and may lean on the bit, instead of engaging its hind legs further under its body.

These same principles also apply to increasing and decreasing the strides in canter.

For both the **collected trot** and the **extended trot** the horse needs to have been well schooled and the rider needs to be skilled and experienced in his use of the aids.

To obtain the collected trot, the rider alternately 'asks' and yields with his hands, and at the same time pushes with his weight and legs, so that the horse steps further forward under its centre of gravity and takes shorter but more deliberate and expressive steps.

Slowing of the trot induced by excessive use of the hands unsupported by the legs is incorrect, as are hovering steps resulting from tension.

Canter

In the canter the horse moves in three-time in a series of leaps, during each of which there is a moment of suspension. Depending on which lateral pair of legs is stepping further forward, the horse is said to be in right or left canter, cantering with the right or left leg leading, or cantering on the right or left leg. Normally, in the school, the horse canters with the inside leg leading. It is then said to be cantering 'true'. If the outside pair of legs is leading, the horse is said to be in 'counter-canter'.

The canter is the only gait in which the horse is flexed when being ridden straight ahead.

The different forms of canter are the working canter, the medium canter, the collected canter and the extended canter.

Before the **transition** or **strike-off into canter,** the rider needs to prepare the horse by performing one or more half-halts to bring the hind feet further forward under the centre of gravity. In this way more weight is transferred onto the hind legs, making it easier for the horse to strike off into the canter.

To strike off into right canter, for example, the aids are as follows:

* prepare the horse with half-halts

* place more weight on the inside seat bone

* use the right leg at the girth to push the horse forwards

* at the same time flex the horse to the right by 'asking' with the right rein

- use the left rein to regulate the amount of flexion and to prevent the horse falling out onto the left shoulder

- place the outside (left) leg in a 'guarding' position about 10cm behind the girth to prevent the left hind leg from stepping sideways and to make sure it steps forward in the direction of the centre of gravity; the role of the rider's outside leg is particularly important, since in the phase of the canter when only one of the horse's hind feet is on the ground, this foot can only bear the weight correctly if it is underneath the centre of gravity

- as soon as the horse strikes of into canter, 'let the stride through' by yielding slightly with the hands, especially the inside one.

The weight and leg aids are then used to push the horse forward and keep the canter going. The rider goes with the movement from his hips, while keeping his upper body as still as possible. The rider's inside hip should be slightly in front of the outside one but the outside shoulder should not be 'left behind'. The seat should remain softly in the saddle and not bump up and down.

> **NOTE** A correct canter depends on the correct position of the rider's legs. The rider should sit each canter stride as if he were asking the horse to strike off afresh into canter.

The hands should keep an even contact with the horse's mouth during the canter. Correct half-halts are particularly important: along with the driving aids they serve to maintain the spring and impulsion and to keep the horse 'together'.

To counteract **crookedness**, the horse can be ridden more from the inside leg to the outside rein (while still maintaining a slight inside flexion). Horses tend to canter 'quarters in', especially when increasing and decreasing the strides in canter.

Working canter

When riding **transitions** from one form of canter to another, the same rules apply as in trot. For example, when 'lengthening the strides' as a preparation for medium canter, a gradual transition in which the strides are lengthened progressively is better than charging forward and quickening the strides.

When lengthening the canter strides, the horse must also lengthen its frame, as in medium trot. Giving away the reins is a good way of checking that the horse is still in self-carriage.

In the **simple change of leg** there should be a clear, and at the same time soft, transition from canter to walk. After three to five well-defined walk steps, the horse should strike off purposefully into canter again. Half-halts should be used to prepare for each transition.

Teaching the horse the beginnings of **collection** in canter entails gradually shortening the strides by means of half-halts. The driving aids cause the hind legs to engage more, and then the 'restraining' element of the half-halt causes more of the weight to be placed on them.

The rider performs the half-halts, i.e. 'asks' and then yields, in time with the canter strides. However, the rein aids should never predominate over the driving aids and they should always be supported by the latter. With more advanced horses, the hands play a more passive role and collection is obtained primarily through the use of the weight and legs. At this (advanced) stage the rider can feel the powerful thrust of the hind legs underneath his seat.

When the canter is shortened by use of the reins alone (especially the inside rein) the result is a tense, shuffling or incorrect canter gait. The diagonally opposite legs which are supposed to be set down as a pair are set down separately: the inside

hind foot is set down before the outside forefoot. The horse is then sometimes said to be cantering 'in four-time'.

The three-time beat of the canter must be conserved at all times and if lost must be re-established by riding actively forward.

In **counter-canter** the horse should not be ridden quite so deeply into the corners. Both the forehand and the hindquarters should remain on the same track, and the horse should be flexed to the side of the leading leg, i.e. to the right in right canter on the left rein, and to the left in left canter on the right rein.

The half-halt and the transition to halt

The half-halt and the halt, that is, the transition to halt, are performed in the same way. They differ only in effect.

Half-halts are used:
* when riding a transition from one gait to another
* to shorten or adjust the strides within a gait
* to alert the horse prior to a new exercise or movement
* to improve or maintain the horse's collection and carriage within a movement.

To perform a half-halt, the rider places more weight on his seat bones by tightening his back muscles, pushes the horse forward with his legs, and uses a carefully measured asking or non-yielding rein aid followed with minimum delay by a yielding rein.

To sum up, it could be said that half-halts consist of a combination of all the aids and are essential for controlled, accurate riding.

> **NOTE** A half-halt consists in briefly 'enclosing' the horse a little more between the weight, leg and rein aids, and then yielding with the reins again.

At the first signs of success, the rider should become lighter in his hands again. If necessary, the half-halt can be repeated several times.

> **NOTE** The half-halt is not a 'one off' action: it should be repeated as often as necessary, i.e. until it has fulfilled its purpose.

The forward-driving element of the half-halt serves to increase the horse's desire to move forward, with the result that it comes more positively onto the bit. A well-schooled horse will then yield to the bit of its own accord, as it were, and if it is sufficiently supple and 'through' *(Durchlässigkeit),* it will also engage its hind legs further under its body as it does so.

The rein aids should never be so strong that they act in a backward direction and 'block' the forward reach of the hind legs. In the half-halt the horse must be able to swing its hind legs forward to their full extent.

If the rein aids in the half-halt are given on only one rein, the other rein should remain quietly in contact, to prevent the bit being pulled sideways through the horse's mouth.

The commonly heard expression 'half-halt on the left, right or outside rein' is misleading since it could imply that the rein alone is used, whereas a correct and meaningful half-halt is only possible if the forward-driving aids are used at the same time. The aims of the half-halt as described above can only be achieved if the hind legs are made to step forward so that horse comes for a moment more positively onto the bit, or, on a curved track, more positively into the outside rein.

The (transition to) **halt** can be performed from any gait. It is performed only on straight lines. It is usually preceded, by way of preparation, by one or more half-halts.

The aids are the same as for the half-halt, except that to obtain the actual halt, the horse is pushed momentarily with the weight and leg aids into a non-yielding hand. How strongly these aids need to be applied depends on the stage of training and the level of understanding between horse and rider. If the halt is properly prepared, it can be performed with the very lightest of aids.

Since in the halt the horse should stand square, with all four feet on the ground and underneath it, and in self-carriage, it is particularly important for the hands to yield, i.e. become lighter, immediately the horse responds, rather than after it has actually come to a halt. The rider should continue to keep the horse lightly 'on the aids' after it has halted, so that it can move off again effortlessly at any time into the required gait.

> **NOTE** In the halt too, the rider needs to keep the horse in front of the leg, i.e. in front of his driving aids.

If, in the halt, the horse steps back with its hind legs, or with all four legs, or if it goes against the bit, this is usually because the rider's hands have remained fixed in position instead of yielding or have not yielded promptly.

Using the halt as an opportunity to adjust tack and clothing is bad practice since it encourages the horse to fidget and come 'off the aids'. It then becomes impossible to make a clear, purposeful transition forward from the halt.

Lateral flexion and bend

The horse is said to be **flexed** when its head is turned sideways from the poll, which is the joint between the head and the neck. The back edge of the lower jawbone slides underneath the parotid gland on the side to which the head is flexed. If the horse is working with looseness *(Losgelassenheit),* the crest will 'flip' over to the side of the flexion.

The horse's longitudinal axis (spine) plays no part in this flexion and remains straight.

The rider uses the flexion to make the horse more obedient to the sideways-acting element of the rein aids. The horse's ability to accept and yield to the inside aids is improved and it learns to go more 'into the outside aids'.

Irrespective of whether the horse is being ridden on the right or the left rein around the school, the side to which it is flexed is known as the 'inside' and the other side as the 'outside'.

To obtain a correct, well-defined flexion, the rider sits with his weight equally distributed over both seat bones and, without giving up the contact with the horse's mouth, yields the outside rein by almost the same amount that he has shortened the inside one. If the horse is flexed correctly, the rider will just be able to see the inside eye and the edge of the nostril.

Attempting to exceed this degree of flexion will almost always result in the horse falling out onto the outside shoulder and losing rhythm.

When changing the flexion from one side to the other (for example, when changing the rein), before flexing the horse in the new direction, the rider must first straighten it properly while continuing to use the forward-driving aids.

The commonest and most serious fault is trying to obtain the flexion by overtightening or pulling the inside rein. This constricts the neck and prevents the horse from stepping forward and under with its inside hind leg.

Another fault is not yielding the outside rein sufficiently to 'allow' the flexion. This leads to **tilting the head** or 'tipping the nose', in which the horse carries its head crookedly with one ear higher than the other.

To correct this fault, the rider should position the horse straight and use positive forward-driving aids to make it stretch to the rein and take it forward and down. Then he can try the flexion again, taking care to use the rein aids tactfully.

However, it is also incorrect to lengthen the outside rein too much. All that happens then is that the head is pulled inwards by the action of the inside rein.

The term **bend** is used when the horse is bent throughout its longitudinal axis, i.e. throughout the whole length of its spine.

The horse's body should be bent as much as is anatomically possible. It cannot be bent uniformly from head to tail, because the degree of flexibility varies with the different types of vertebra. The part of the spine in front of the withers is the most flexible, the section made up of the cervical vertebrae is less so, and the sacrum is completely rigid because the sacral vertebrae are fused together.

Bearing this in mind, the rider should avoid asking for too much bend in the head and neck and should concentrate on getting the horse to bend adequately through the ribs, around his inside leg.

What flexibility there is must be exploited to the full in order to increase

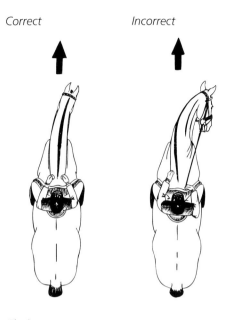

Correct   Incorrect

Flexion

the horse's suppleness, prevent the hindquarters swinging on turns and also to enable the horse to be straightened properly.

However, to bend correctly, the horse must first have learned to accept and 'go into' the outside rein.

NOTE Although their value is often underestimated, the outside aids have a particularly important part to play in flexing and bending the horse.

The bend is obtained by finely balanced and coordinated **diagonal aids**. The procedure is as follows:

* more weight is placed on the inside seat bone

* the inside leg next to the girth encourages the inside hind leg to step forwards

* the outside leg is placed in a 'guarding' position about 10cm behind the girth to prevent the quarters swinging out

* the inside rein keeps the horse flexed and soft, and may also 'lead' the horse into the turn

* the outside rein yields sufficiently to allow the flexion or bend to the inside, prevents excessive bend in the head and neck, and prevents the shoulder falling out.

There can be no bend without flexion, whereas it is possible, and sometimes necessary, for the horse to be flexed without being bent, for example, in certain exercises such as leg-yielding.

Riding turns and curved or circular tracks

Turns and curved or circular tracks can only be ridden correctly if the horse is

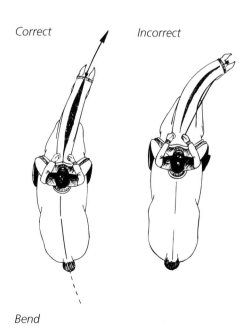

Correct   Incorrect

Bend

reliably and consistently 'on the aids' and can be bent throughout its length, as far as is anatomically possible, in accordance with the curvature of the track it is following. The hind legs should follow in the same track as the forelegs, and the inside hind leg is required to carry an increased share of the weight.

> **NOTE** On curved tracks the hind legs should be aligned with the forelegs, i.e. the hind feet should follow the same tracks as the fore feet. This is known as being 'straight to the track on the circle' or 'straight to the track in the turn', etc.

Every **corner** should be ridden as an exercise in its own right and is a test of the horse's suppleness. A corner is ridden as a quarter circle or quarter volte and the horse should be bent accordingly.

How deep the horse is ridden into the corner depends on its level of training and on the radius of the quarter circle or volte. In Germany, at novice level (Class 'A'), the corner should be ridden as a quarter of a 10m circle (5m radius), at elementary level (Class 'E') as a quarter of an 8m circle (4m radius), and at all levels above this as a

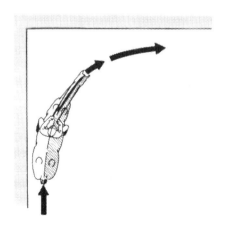

Riding through a corner.

quarter of a 6m circle, or 'volte' (3m radius).

The rider performs a half-halt before the corner and flexes the horse in the direction of the movement, i.e. to the inside. The diagonal aids create the longitudinal bend required for riding through the corner.

The novice rider can start off by riding accurately through the corner in walk. This way he has more time to practise the aids. The forehand should not be pushed too far into the corner. Another fault is trying to make the horse go into the corner by carrying both hands, especially the inside one, to the outside. This causes the horse to fall out onto the outside shoulder. If the horse tries to cut the corner, the rider should counteract this tendency by using his inside aids more strongly. When there is not an outside wall, the rider should ensure that the horse does not fall onto its outside shoulder and escape sideways before the corner.

When **changing the rein across the diagonal** the rider should use the inside leg and the outside rein to ensure that the horse does not turn off the track too early. The turn should not begin until the horse's shoulder is level with the marker. Across the diagonal the horse should remain in front of the legs, should be straight, and should work into both reins equally. The shoulder should again be level with the marker when the horse rejoins the track on the other side of the school.

On the **circle** the horse should be ridden with a constant bend. The aids are as described above, i.e. the inside leg, next to the girth, makes the inside hind foot step forward, maintains the bend, and prevents the horse falling in on the circle. The outside leg is in a 'guarding' position behind the girth and, along with the outside rein, prevents the horse from falling out and ensures that the outside hind foot

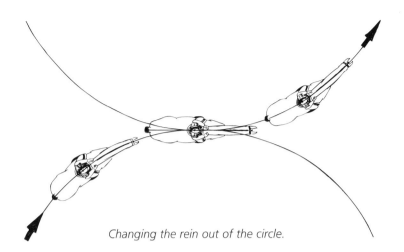

Changing the rein out of the circle.

steps forward correctly and evenly.

When **changing the bend** (for example, when changing the rein out of or through the circle and when riding serpentines), the horse should be ridden straight for a few metres before being bent in the new direction. When the horse becomes more supple and 'through' *(Durchlässigkeit),* as required for two-loop serpentines on the long side and for figures of eight, it will make a smooth, elastic transition from the bent to the straight position. Only when the horse is straight should the rider change the diagonal in trot and flex the horse in the new direction. He should then also move his weight slightly to what will be the 'new' inside and adjust his leg position and his reins.

Frequent changes of bend are good for the education of both horse and rider. However, they need to be performed correctly, i.e. the **change of diagonal**, the rider's **change of position**, and the **change of flexion and bend** need to be accomplished smoothly, elastically and deliberately.

Circles of 10m diameter and less, require the maximum bend of which the horse is capable. The forehand should be aligned with the hindquarters, i.e. the circle should be on a single track. These circles can be ridden anywhere in the arena. In basic training, they are 10m in diameter and are ridden in working trot. As training progresses, the diameter is reduced to 8m and finally to a minimum of 6m. A 6m circle is called a **volte**, and is ridden only in collected gaits because it requires a high degree of bend. If the diameter of the circle is reduced below 6m, the horse has difficulty bending sufficiently to stay on the track, with the result that its quarters swing out and it loses rhythm.

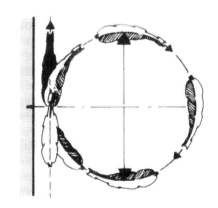

Volte or small circle

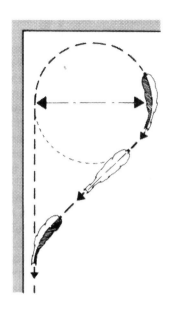

Half circle or half volte and return to track.

A common fault is an elliptical or egg-shaped circle or volte. The two halves of the circle should be of equal size and the circle should start and end at the same place.

The **half circle and return to track** can be performed part way along the long side or out of the corner (usually the second corner of the long side). The first part is ridden as half of a small circle. When it reaches the point of the circle which is furthest away from the long side, the horse is ridden obliquely back to the track in a straight line. It arrives back at the track on the opposite rein.

When riding turns and circles, especially small circles and voltes, the rider should beware of using the inside rein too strongly. He should also ensure that the elastic contact on the outside rein is maintained, otherwise there is a tendency for the horse to come behind the vertical or lose rhythm.

Serpentines along the long side can be made up of one or two loops. In a

single-loop serpentine, the deepest point of the loop is level with the half marker on the long side, and in the two-loop serpentine the deepest points are level with the quarter markers. In the single-loop serpentine the loop is 5m deep, and in the two-loop serpentine the loops are 2.5m deep. In serpentines, the flexion and bend need to be changed after every turn. Serpentines are ridden in working or collected gaits.

Serpentines through the whole school, depending on the number of loops and their width, help to develop looseness *(Losgelassenheit)* or to prepare the horse for collection. The number of loops depends on the size of the school and the level of training of the rider and of the horse. They always begin and end half way along the short side at A or C. In a 20m x 40m arena the number of loops is usually either three or four.

In dressage tests, the serpentine through the whole school consists of several small half circles of equal size with a straight section in between. The length of the straight section depends on the number, and so the diameter, of the loops. In this sort of serpentine, the horse is straightened at the end of each loop, and then bent again at the beginning of the next half circle. The horse finishes on the same rein if there is an odd number of loops, and on the opposite rein if there is an even number of loops. Changing the diagonal in trot or changing the leg in canter should take place when crossing the centre line (see diagrams on pages 16 and 17).

In another type of serpentine, which is not used in tests, each loop is joined directly onto the next, without a straight section. This type of serpentine begins and ends at the quarter markers. The horse crosses the centre line at an angle

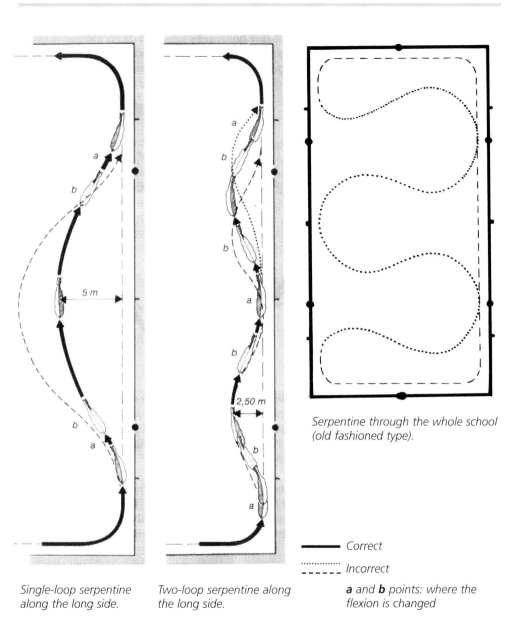

Single-loop serpentine along the long side.

Two-loop serpentine along the long side.

Serpentine through the whole school (old fashioned type).

——— *Correct*

·········· *Incorrect*

- - - - *Incorrect*

a and b points: where the flexion is changed

so that the loops are pear-shaped (see diagram). The flexion and bend are changed smoothly as the horse crosses the centre line. This serpentine helps to promotes skilful riding, as well as making the horse more supple and 'through' (*Durchlässigkeit*). In fact it is a valuable suppling exercise for both horse and rider.

The half turn on the forehand

Turns from a halt can be either around the forehand or around the haunches. The centre point of the turn is next to the horse's inside forefoot in the turn on the forehand, and next to the inside hind foot in the turn on the haunches.

The **half turn on the forehand** is an exercise aimed at developing looseness *(Losgelassenheit)* and also serves to teach the horse to respond to the sideways-pushing aids. Since the exercise is performed slowly, and can be taken 'a step at a time' if necessary, it is a good opportunity for the young or novice rider to learn and practise each aid, and above all to learn to coordinate the aids.

The half turn on the forehand is performed as follows:

* the horse is halted; so as to avoid making the horse step back or raise its head, when riding in an enclosed area the turn on the forehand should be performed on the inside track, and not up against the wall

* the horse is flexed to the side of the sideways-pushing leg, i.e. in the direction of the turn

* the inside hind foot steps in front of and across the outside hind foot

* at the end of the exercise, i.e. when the horse has turned through 180°, it is positioned straight again in the halt; at this point it will be back on the outside track.

The following aids are used for the turn on the forehand:

* in order to obtain the flexion, the rider transfers more of his weight onto the inside seat bone and shortens the new inside rein

* the outside 'guarding' rein prevents excessive bend in the head and neck

* with his inside leg drawn back slightly, the rider pushes the hindquarters, step by step, forwards and sideways around the forehand; he uses his leg in time with the horse's movement

* the outside 'guarding' leg prevents the

The individual phases of the turn on the forehand.

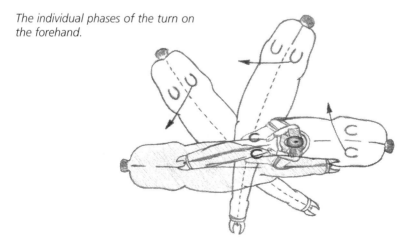

horse from stepping too far sideways and prevents the movement from becoming hurried

* at the end of the movement the horse is halted again.

Throughout the turn the rider must use his legs and weight to keep the horse 'in front of the leg'. This is the only way to ensure that the horse will remain on the bit and will not escape forwards or step back.

Leg-yielding

Leg-yielding is an exercise aimed at developing looseness *(Losgelassenheit)* and in particular at making the horse more responsive to the sideways-pushing aids. It is an excellent exercise for teaching the rider to coordinate the aids.

In leg-yielding the horse is slightly flexed laterally, but not bent, and moves forward on two tracks. The inside feet step regularly and evenly in front of and across the outside feet. The flexion is always to the side of the sideways-pushing leg. The sideways-pushing leg is therefore the inside leg, even when it is on the side closest to the wall. Leg-yielding is usually performed in walk, although with more advanced riders on appropriate horses it may be ridden in working trot. It should only be ridden for short periods at a time.

The aids for leg-yielding are as follows:

* the rider places more weight on the inside seat bone

* the inside leg is positioned just behind the girth and pushes **forwards** and sideways, keeping as far as possible in time with the movement

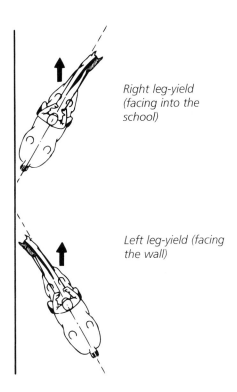

Right leg-yield (facing into the school)

Left leg-yield (facing the wall)

* the outside leg is placed in a 'guarding' position behind the girth, preventing the horse from moving its hindquarters too far sideways; it is also responsible for maintaining the forward movement

* the rider 'feels' the inside rein in order to obtain the flexion

* he 'gives' sufficiently with the outside rein to allow the flexion while still maintaining a steady contact with the horse's mouth. He also uses the outside rein to prevent the horse bending its head and neck excessively and falling out onto the outside shoulder.

It is easier for the novice rider to start with the leg-yield along the wall and with the head to the wall. He can then concentrate on his sideways-pushing aids and does not need to use his rein aids so much because the wall is there to help him.

Later in the training it is more beneficial, though more difficult, to perform the leg-yield with the head to the inside of the school.

The leg-yield should be performed with the horse at a maximum angle of 45° to the track. If the angle is increased, the horse goes sideways instead of forwards and sideways, and loses rhythm, as well as possibly damaging its legs.

When riding the leg-yield with the head to the wall, the rider finishes the exercise by changing to the opposite flexion and riding the horse forward on a shallow curved track until its hindquarters are back on the outside track. When riding the leg-yield with the head to the inside, the rider finishes by realigning the forehand with the quarters without changing the flexion.

Leg-yielding away from and back to the track consists of performing the leg-yield diagonally across the school and back again. This exercise requires a higher degree of suppleness *(Durchlässigkeit),* and greater precision and skill in the use of the aids. As in the leg-yield along the wall, the horse moves on two tracks and is flexed away from the direction of the movement. The exercise is performed in walk, and in working trot if the rider is sufficiently experienced.

The exercise begins at the first marker along the long side. After riding through the corner, the rider has several metres within which to flex the horse before arriving at the marker. He should then apply the aids so that the horse steps forwards and sideways along the intended diagonal line while always remaining parallel to the long side. The hindquarters should not hurry and lead the forehand. On arriving at the quarter line, i.e. about 5m from the outside track, the horse is straightened and ridden forward for a

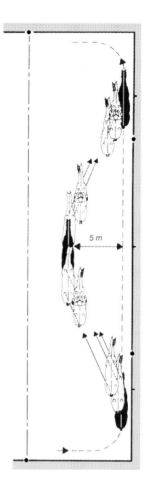

Leg-yielding away from and back to the track.

(horse's) length in the straight position. The rider then flexes it to the opposite side and leg-yields diagonally back to the track along the intended path.

The exercise finishes at the last marker along the long side. Leg-yielding on diagonal lines should not be attempted until the horse has mastered the leg-yield along the wall.

Rein-back

The rein-back serves to develop and test the horse's suppleness and ability to 'let

Rein-back

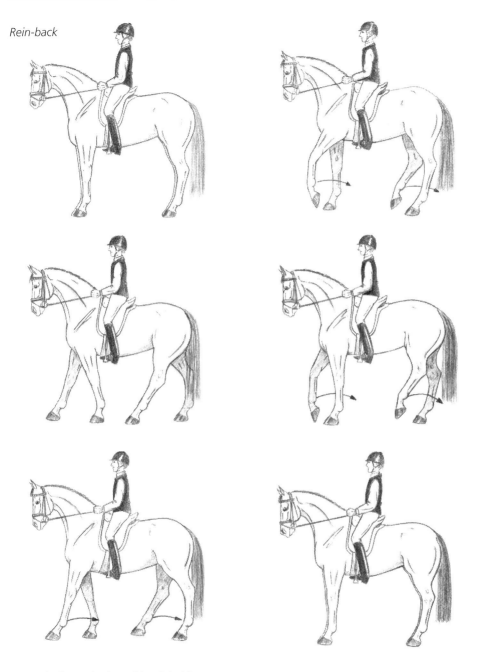

the aids through' *(Durchlässigkeit).*
Moreover, it helps to improve the
collection since it causes the joints of the
hind legs and quarters to bend more. It
can also be used as an exercise in
obedience.

The horse steps back in clearly defined
diagonal two-time. It should step back
calmly and in a straight line. The feet
should be picked up cleanly and the strides
should be of equal length.

During basic training the horse is asked

to rein back for a specified distance (e.g one length, which equals three to four steps). Only at a later stage is a set number of steps required. If the rein-back is to end in a halt, the last step of rein-back will actually be a half step, though it counts as a full step. As a result of this half step, the horse finishes standing square.

Before attempting the rein-back, the horse must be standing straight and square and well 'on the aids' with its weight distributed evenly on all four legs. The aids are then as follows:

* the rider uses his weight (on both seat bones) and legs as if to send the horse forward

* the rider's lower legs are placed in a 'guarding' position to prevent the horse moving its hindquarters sideways

* the moment the horse responds and goes to step forwards, the rider 'feels' both reins, i.e. gives an asking rein aid; at a more advanced stage of training, a non-yielding rein aid is used instead – in either case the forward energy which has been created is converted into backward movement

* as soon as the horse responds by starting to move backwards, the rider's hands become light again, although they must still keep a contact with the horse's mouth.

With horses that find the rein-back particularly difficult, it is sometimes helpful to take some of the weight off the horse's back. The rider should not lean forward, however, since unless he is sitting upright he is not in a position to send the horse forward out of the rein-back at any point or prevent it from rushing backwards, by 'tightening his back muscles', pushing the horse forward with his legs and yielding with his hands.

The half turn on the haunches and the half pirouette

The half turn on the haunches is an exercise for improving collection. It is a demanding movement for both horse and rider.

From a well-established, steady halt, with a good contact and a slight lateral flexion, the horse describes a half circle with its forehand around its hindquarters. The centre point of the circle is as close as possible to the horse's inside hind foot. The inside hind foot steps up and down in the walk rhythm. The outside hind foot describes a small half circle around the inside hind foot. The forefeet step forwards and sideways and cross one in front of the other. The hind feet should not cross.

Because the position of the centre of the circle is next to the inside hind foot, the horse moves onto a slightly different track, the width of its body away from the original track. It must therefore finish the movement by taking a step sideways, back onto the original track. This is the only point in the movement when the outside hind foot is allowed to step sideways across the inside one.

Before starting the movement, the horse must have completed a successful transition to halt.

The aids for the half turn on the haunches are as follows:

* the rider places more weight on the inside seat bone

* the horse is flexed in the direction of the movement

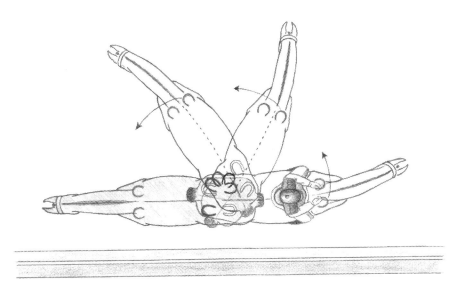

The individual phases of the turn on the haunches.

• the rider's inside leg is positioned close to the girth, in a forward-driving position; along with the outside leg, which is in the 'guarding' position, it is used to create the bend and at the same time to keep the hind feet moving in the walk rhythm and stepping forward slightly under the horse's body; the inside leg can also be used to prevent the inside hind foot from stepping to the inside

• the outside leg is the 'guarding' leg – it should never exert a sideways-pushing action, because this would cause the hind legs to cross and the inside hind leg to step inwards; the outside leg is also jointly responsible for maintaining the impulsion

• the inside rein, which can exert a slightly sideways action, leads the horse into the turn

• the outside rein prevents excessive bend, but 'gives' sufficiently to allow the horse to move as required in the direction of the turn.

With novice riders it is a good idea to let the horse take a step or two forwards and then enter the turn from the forward movement. Stepping forward slightly is the least serious fault in the turn on the haunches. Stepping backwards, on the other hand, indicates that the horse is evading the forward-driving aids and that the rider is using the reins incorrectly.

At the end of the turn, the horse should be straight and standing calmly on the original track with its weight evenly distributed on all four legs.

If the horse finds the turn difficult, the rider should repeat the exercise, riding the horse forward more. Touching it on the outside shoulder with the whip can also be helpful. On no account should the rider attempt to push the horse around with the outside rein, since this would restrict the forward movement and the bend.

The rider can prevent the horse turning too fast by performing a half-halt with the inside leg and outside hand. Riding two or three strides of the turn at frequent intervals, and then riding straight ahead again, is a useful exercise for improving the horse's obedience to the leg.

The **half pirouette** is performed out of the medium walk or from trot. In the latter case, the horse performs a transition to walk just before beginning the turn, i.e. the actual turn is ridden in walk. The half pirouette is performed in the same way as the turn on the haunches except that the horse does not halt at the beginning or end.

The aids are the same as for the turn on the haunches. However, the rider needs to prepare the horse more with half-halts beforehand. If the horse is in trot, the first stage consists in performing the transition to walk. The horse then takes, at most, one step forward, makes a turn around its hindquarters, and goes immediately forward to trot with no intermediate walk steps.

With horses which are very sensitive to the sideways-pushing aids, it is a good idea to 'think shoulder-in' during the last few steps before the turn.

This exercise can also be ridden with 60° or 90° of turn. The latter is known as a 'quarter pirouette'.

Order of performing and training the basic dressage movements

* Loose rein and long rein walk.

* Riding-in: exercises for obtaining and developing looseness (Losgelassenheit).

In the main part of the lesson, a selection of exercises and movements can be performed, depending on the horse's level of training. The aim of this work is to make the horse more supple and 'through' (Durchlässigkeit). Some exercises which increase the horse's engagement and help develop collection are:

* strike off into canter from walk
* small circles in trot
* transitions from trot to halt
* rein-back
* medium trot and medium canter – with frequent transitions from medium to working trot/canter, and back again.

With more experienced horses and riders, more advanced exercises can be included in this phase, for example:

* transitions from canter to walk
* counter-canter
* small circles in canter
* simple change of leg in canter
* extended trot and canter with frequent transitions from extended to working or collected trot/canter, and back again
* half turn on the haunches and half pirouette.

Final phase: relaxation and cooling down.

Working as a ride and riding quadrilles

Working in a ride is not just a way to practise dressage movements in the company of other horses and riders. It is also a test of the rider's skill since he needs to be able to ride the horse accurately in order to keep his position in the ride at the same time as maintaining the correct gait and the appropriate form of the gait (working, medium, etc.). Hence working in a ride is also a particularly useful exercise for young horses since it tests their responsiveness and obedience and is also a good preparation for taking part in competitions.

For team rides and quadrilles, an understanding of the school commands is essential. The ride is first given advance warning, and then given the definitive command, for example, 'Ride prepare to walk… Ride walk'. There is a short pause in between to give the riders time to prepare their horses. The definitive command is given when all the riders have enough room to carry out the command and are at the appropriate points in the arena.

When working in a ride, it is essential that the distances between the horses are equal when riding one behind the other, and that the lateral spacings are equal when riding side by side.

Command	*Response*	*Remarks*
Forming a ride		
On the right (left) rein, in walk (trot/canter), form a ride behind X (name of leading file).	Form a ride in single file. The rider named as leading file rides onto the outside track in walk, trot or canter as instructed, raises his right hand and calls out 'front of the ride'. The other riders fall in behind the leading file in a pre-arranged order, or as instructed.	
Transitions		
Ride, prepare to go forward to walk… Ride, walk march.	Transition from halt to walk.	The definitive command (as opposed to the instruction to 'Prepare to …') is given with the leading file positioned just before the first corner of the short side so that the ride will find it easier to keep together.
Ride, prepare to go forward to medium walk… Ride, walk.	Downward transition to walk.	
Ride, prepare to go forward to working canter… Ride, canter.	Transition into working canter from another gait.	
Ride, prepare to go forward to medium trot… Ride, medium trot.		

Command	Response	Remarks

Transitions (continued)

Ride, prepare to go forward to working (collected) trot/canter... Ride, working (collected) trot/canter.

Downward transition from medium trot or canter to working or collected trot or canter.

Ride, prepare to go forward to halt... Ride, halt.

Ride, prepare to rein-back 3 metres... Ride, rein-back

Lining up at the halt

Leading file, turning right across the school, the others lining up on the left, 3m spaces... Leading file right turn ... Halt.

The ride is on the right rein. On the command 'Right turn', the leading file turns off the outside track at a right angle into the school, and crosses towards the other side in a straight line. The other riders each ride one horse's length beyond the point at which the previous horse has turned, and then turn also. On the command 'Halt', the leading file halts his horse at 90° to the opposite track. The other riders continue in the same gait until level with the croup of the horse on their right, and then continue forward in walk until level with the lead rider.

Whole ride prepare to turn left and halt... Ride, left turn... Ride, halt.

The ride is on the left rein. On the command 'Left turn 'all the riders turn

Command	Response	Remarks

Lining up at the halt (continued)

simultaneously off the outside track at a right angle. On the command 'Halt', they all halt simultaneously, with the horses at a right angle to the long side and level with each other.

Moving off from the halt

Ride, forward to the track and right turn... Ride, walk march.

The ride is lined up facing the long side with the horses' noses level with the centre line.

The rider at the end of the line on the right (No.1) rides straight ahead in walk; the second rider waits until the first horse's croup is about a length ahead of his horse's head, and then he also rides forward. The other riders do the same, riding straight ahead and turning onto the track through a quarter volte to fall in behind the leading rider. There is then a distance of two lengths between horses.

If the horses are standing close together, i.e. without the 3m spacing between them, there will be only one length between them when they reach the track.

School figures and changing the rein

Whole ride prepare to turn right... Right turn.

All the riders simultaneously make a 90° right turn.

Command	Response	Remarks

School figures and changing the rein (continued)

Command	Response	Remarks
Change the rein across the diagonal/short diagonal.		The command is given before the first rider reaches the second corner of the short side.
Change the rein down the centre line.		The command is given when the first rider is approaching the second corner of the long side.
In single file: turn across the centre of the school… go large… circle…	All the riders in the ride follow the same track or ride the same figure, one behind the other. 'Going large' means following the outside track.	
On two circles.	The first rider turns onto a circle at the next circle point. The other riders follow when they reach the same point. The second group of riders turns off onto an adjoining circle in the opposite direction. The two leading files should be opposite each other, giving a 'mirror image' effect.	The lead rider of the second circle should be designated in advance.
Change the rein out of the circle(s).	When riding on adjoining circles, each rider passes and changes the rein behind the approaching rider from the opposite circle.	

Command	Response	Remarks

School figures and changing the rein (continued)

Command	Response	Remarks
In single file (or: leading file followed by the rest of the ride), change the rein through the circle.	At the circle point before the open side of the circle(the point where the circle turns away from the long side towards the centre of the school), the leading file turns into the circle and rides a half circle on each rein, passing through the centre of the circle and arriving on the opposite track at the circle point before the open side of the new circle.	
In single file, serpentine one loop (two loops) along the long side. Or, in single file, serpentine through the whole school, … loops.	The first rider begins the serpentine after the first corner of the long side. The flexion and bend are changed on beginning each loop or turn.	The commands are given before the first corner of the long side. The number of loops depends on the size of the school and the level of training of horse and rider.
Whole ride, volte (or 6m, 8m or 10m circle), now.	On the command 'now', all the riders turn off the track individually onto a volte or small circle, returning to the track at the same point that they left it.	
Whole ride, half volte (half circle), now.	All the riders turn off the track individually onto a half volte, or half circle, and then incline back to the track. In the case of a 10m circle, for example, they return to it 15m behind the point where they turned off it.	The command is given so that the first rider performs the half circle or volte in the last corner of the long side.

Command	Response	Remarks

School figures and changing the rein (continued)

Command	Response	Remarks
In single file, in the corner, half volte (half circle).	The half volte, or half of a small circle, is performed by the all the riders, one behind the other.	The command is given before the last corner of the long side.
Whole ride, right (left) quarter turn (half turn) on the forehand… Ride, turn (about turn).	All the riders perform simultaneously a quarter turn (90°) or half turn (180°) on the forehand.	In an enclosed school, the exercise must be performed on an inside track (1m in from the outside track). Command: 'Onto the inside track'.
Whole ride, right (left) quarter turn (half turn) on the haunches… Ride, turn (about turn).	All the riders simultaneously perform a 90° or 180° turn on the haunches (from the halt).	
Whole ride, half pirouette… Ride, about turn.	All the riders perform simultaneously a half turn about the haunches from the walk.	
On (for example) the next long side, right (left) leg-yield for half of the long side.	Each rider begins the leg-yield at the same point as the previous rider and ends it at the same point.	When the command is given to finish, all the riders should stop leg-yielding at the same time. This also applies if the exercise is ended prematurely.
Leg-yield into the school and back to the track.	The riders follow one behind the other, on the same track. At the half marker each rider should each be about 5m in from the track.	

3.3 Basic Jumping Exercises for the Rider

Before the rider begins his basic training in jumping, certain criteria need to be met in order to ensure safe and accident-free progress:

* As well as the correct tack (e.g. jumping or general-purpose saddle) and a hard hat, a neckstrap can be used to give the novice rider extra support.

* In addition to the basic seat, the rider must have learned to ride and keep his balance in the various forms of the light seat which are used in different situations.

* He must be able to keep his horse 'on the aids' when riding in the light seat.

The light seat can be practised on the lunge and in the school as well as outside. Riding up and down slopes is particularly good for developing the rider's balance,

and for teaching him to fold forward from the hips and go with the horse's movement. If the foundations are laid correctly, i.e. the rider sits elastically and in balance in the light seat, he will later be able to 'go with' the horse correctly over the jump.

Cavalletti

Riding over cavalletti serves as a preparation for jumping. It is an excellent gymnastic exercise for both horse and rider. Cavalletti are poles 2.5m to 3.5m in length, with 'X' shaped supports about 40cm high attached at their ends. The height of the pole depends on which side of the 'X' is on the ground: in the low position the pole is almost on the ground, in the medium position it is about 25cm high, and in the highest position about 40cm high.

The horse is ridden first in walk, and then in trot, over single poles or several poles in a row. The rider uses the light seat in order to take some of the weight off

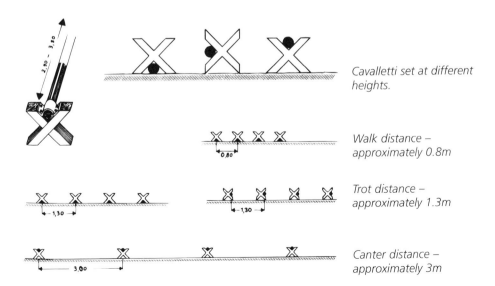

Cavalletti set at different heights.

Walk distance – approximately 0.8m

Trot distance – approximately 1.3m

Canter distance – approximately 3m

the horse's back. The rhythm remains the same before, over and after the cavalletti. As he rides over the poles, the rider 'gives' sufficiently with his hands to allow the horse to stretch its head and neck forward and downward as required. He remains more or less passive and 'goes with' the bigger strides (he will be able to feel the increased activity of the horse's back) by flexing in his hip, knee and ankle joints.

When the rider becomes more proficient and secure in the saddle, he can start riding in a steady, controlled canter over cavalletti in the high position, starting with a single cavalletto, then progressing to a row. When he is able to remain supple and balanced over cavalletti in the light seat, he can start to learn to ride over jumps.

He should start by jumping **single small jumps** out of trot, possibly with a placing pole. The distance between the placing pole and the jump should be about 2-2.2m. Placing poles make it easier for the horse to take off at the right point and allow the rider to concentrate on his seat and position. During this phase of the training attention should be paid to the following points:

* the height of the jumps should be in keeping with the rider's level of training and his confidence

* the jumps should have wings, to deter the horse from running out

* the approach should be ridden straight and to the centre of the jump

* the rider should keep a steady rhythm during the approach

* the horse should remain under control after the jump.

> **NOTE** Only if the rider can ride correctly in the light seat can he be sure of being able to 'go with' the horse before, during and after the jump.

Grids

After a few lessons spent jumping small single fences, rows of jumps can be introduced. The single jump with a placing pole in front of it is gradually developed into a **grid** by the addition of one, and later two or more jumps. The distances between the jumps should be exactly right for the horse. The rider does not need to concentrate too much on the approach and so it is easier for him to follow elastically the rapidly alternating sequence of movements. The rider's suppleness and skill are improved and he learns to keep his lower legs and knees firmly in position and against the horse. Grids help build the rider's confidence and develop his feel for rhythm.

At a later stage in the training, the distances between the jumps in the grid can be varied, and jumps of different sizes and types can be used. This adds variety and extends the rider's experience.

Bounce fences are also good for improving the rider's skill and suppleness. They may be incorporated into grids. A bounce fence consists of two jumps positioned close together so that, immediately after landing, the horse pushes off again energetically with its hindfeet to jump the second half of the fence without taking a canter stride in between.

Single fences

Once the rider is proficient at jumping grids, he can begin jumping **single fences**

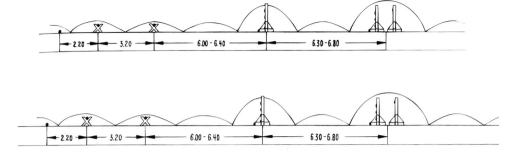

Two examples of grids. (Further examples can be found in Section 4.6)

from a canter. The fences should be straightforward and inviting, and wings should be used.

To begin with, placing poles should be used and the fences jumped from trot. Next, a cavalletto in the medium or high position should be placed about 6m in front of the jump (the exact distance depends on the size of the horse and its length of stride). This positions the horse for the correct take-off from canter.

On the approach, the rider keeps the horse in front of his legs and driving aids, and maintains a steady rhythm in the canter. Pushing the horse hard or checking it sharply before the fence are incorrect and go against the principle that the horse should jump harmoniously out of a rhythmical canter.

For the rider to learn to jump successfully, not only must he first learn the light seat but also he must also learn to ride a correct approach. It is for the instructor to decide when the student is ready to jump single fences out of canter.

The rider should keep the horse 'on the aids' at all times, and **after the jump** the horse should be ridden away in a straight line or on the prescribed track. The rider can also be given exercises, such as turns and transitions, to perform after landing. The aim of these is to improve the horse's suppleness and at the same time to

increase the rider's level of skill.

Jumping exercises can also be performed as part of a dressage or general schooling session as a means of adding variety and teaching the riders and horses to accept jumping as a normal, everyday occurrence.

In jumping lessons, it is not the number of jumps which is important but the correct preparation and judging how much to ask of horse and rider. The instructor should never make excessive demands on horse or rider: both should continue to take pleasure in their work and their safety should not be jeopardised.

Combinations and related distances

Jumping **combinations** is the next stage in the training. Combinations consist of two or three fences or 'elements' between which the horse takes one or two canter strides. A two-fence combination is known as a 'double', and a three-fence combination as a 'treble'. The distance between the elements is approximately 7-8m (one stride in between) or 10-11m (two strides in between).

In combinations, the length of stride and the take-off point for the first fence should be gauged to enable the horse to take the correct number of strides

The distances are measured on the ground from the base of one fence (on the landing side) to the base of the next fence (on the take-off side).

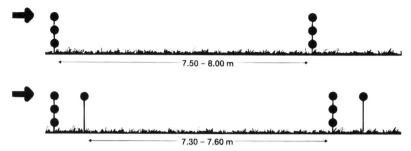

Double, or two-fence combination with one canter stride in between fences.

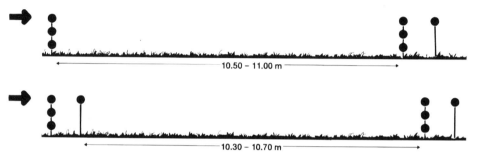

Double, or two-fence combination with two canter strides in between fences.

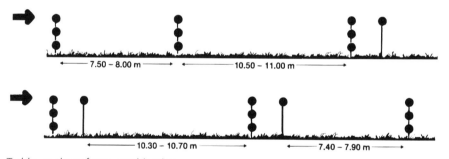

Treble, or three-fence combination.

between fences. However, the rider should be aware that certain factors can make the fences seem closer together or further apart and the distances seem shorter or longer, for example:

* In an outdoor arena, the horse will canter more actively and will take more ground-covering strides than in an indoor school.

* When jumping in the direction of the exit or the stables, most horses cover more ground than when jumping in the opposite direction.

* Horses take more ground-covering strides on firm (but not hard) going. In deep going, especially (loose) uncompacted sand, each stride covers less ground.

• In outdoor arenas any slope must be taken into account: horses cover less ground going uphill than downhill.

• The take-off and landing points depend on the height of the jump.

In addition, the path that the horse describes through the air over the fence, and so also the take-off and landing points, depend on the **type of fence** (upright, spread, etc.).

Once the horse and rider are proficient at jumping small combinations, more difficult fences can gradually be introduced.

There is said to be a **related distance** between fences when the distance corresponds to 3, 4, 5 or 6 canter strides.

The following are the distances used for the different numbers of strides:
• 3 canter strides: approx. 14m to 15m
• 4 canter strides: approx. 17.5m to 18.5m
• 5 canter strides: approx. 21m to 22m
• 6 canter strides: approx. 24.5m to 25.5m

The track between the fences, and so the line along which the related distance is measured, can be straight or curved. For novice riders, a distance measured in a straight line is easier to deal with. For more experienced riders, the advantage of the curved line is that the rider can take a shorter or longer path as desired.

Related distances should be ridden in the **basic canter** used for jumping. The **rhythm** should be maintained. The rider should not check the horse sharply or drive it forward excessively. Obviously he should keep the horse in front of the leg, i.e. in front of the driving aids, and he should be able to send it energetically forward if required.

Varying the number of strides can be an excellent exercise for rider and horse. The rider should already be capable of controlling and adjusting the length of the canter strides when riding on the flat, on a level surface, and he should at the same time be able to keep the horse consistently 'on the aids'.

The following are examples of possible exercises:

• shortening the horse after the first jump and putting in an extra canter stride

• pushing the horse forward more after

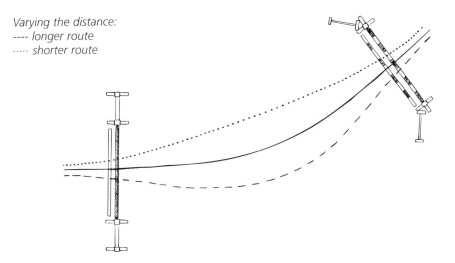

Varying the distance:
---- longer route
····· shorter route

the first jump and putting in one less stride

• when the jumps are not in a straight line, increasing the number of strides by turning wider while maintaining the same length of stride

• when the jumps are not in a straight line, decreasing the number of strides by 'cutting the corner' while still maintaining the same length of stride.

Riding related distances requires good coordination of the aids and sharpens the rider's reactions. It also further develops his feel for rhythm and for a good, active basic canter. It teaches him to ride an accurate track, using a set number of canter strides.

In the early stages, counting the strides out loud in between fences may help the rider to gauge the approach correctly.

Riding a course of jumps

When the above exercises have been mastered, sections of courses can be practised. Basic 'style-jumping test' courses (as run in Germany) are particularly suitable for this purpose. These tests consist of set courses, and

Test No 4
(from the Handbuch für Reit- und Fahrvereine)

Basic style-jumping test

20 x 40m arena (minimum)

Requirements:
After fence 2, at a predetermined point, ride a transition to trot then (rising trot, then sitting trot on the approach to fence 3a).

After fence 3b, continue in right canter over fence 4, continue over the rest of the course.

On crossing the finish, ride a transition to trot (rising), and on a predetermined track (broken line), change the rein diagonally across the school, take sitting trot, then ride a transition to walk and let the horse take the rein forward and down.

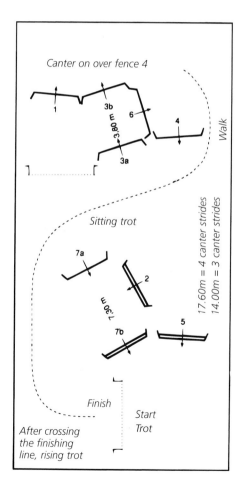

Canter on over fence 4

Walk

Sitting trot

17.60m = 4 canter strides
14.00m = 3 canter strides

3,80 m

3,80 m

Finish

After crossing the finishing line, rising trot

Start
Trot

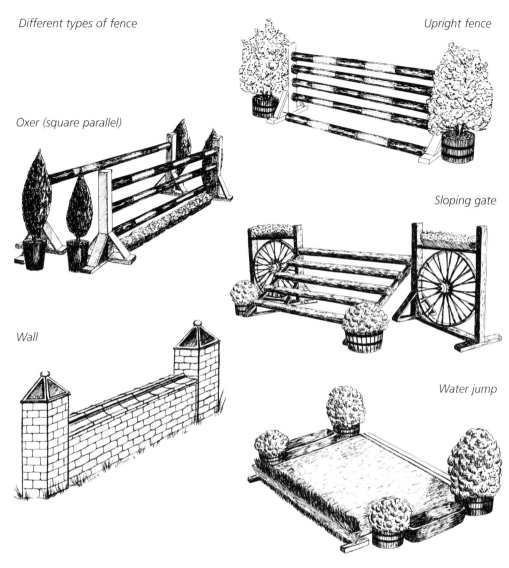

Different types of fence

Upright fence

Oxer (square parallel)

Sloping gate

Wall

Water jump

as well as individual fences, they contain combinations and related distances, and require turns, changes of rein and transitions. Cavalletti are also included in the course, in between the jumps. As well as developing suppleness (Durchlässigkeit), they help to ensure that the course is ridden calmly and steadily.

In these tests the judges are looking for controlled riding in the light seat before and after the jump, good coordination of the aids, suppleness (Durchlässigkeit) in the horse, and overall harmony.

Some guidelines for riding the course are as follows:

* The fences should be approached in the basic canter, which varies slightly from one horse to another. The strides should be even and regular. The horse should approach in a rhythm, take off at the correct point, jump the centre of the fence, and land straight.

* When riding related distances, the rider should ensure that the rhythm is maintained and that the horse takes the correct number of strides. He must be able to lengthen the canter strides on a short-striding horse, or shorten them in the case of a long-striding horse, without losing the rhythm. The number of strides should be as specified, whatever the horse's natural length of stride.

* When riding a combination, the first element should be approached and jumped accordingly, and the horse should then continue smoothly and harmoniously into the second, taking the correct number of strides.

Turns are ridden in canter, on the correct leg and in a rhythm. The rider increases the weight on his inside knee and seat bone. In turns, the outside aids, i.e. the outside regulating leg and rein, are important, since they prevent the horse's outside shoulder and hindleg from falling out.

If the horse knows how to do **flying changes** the rider will quickly learn to make it change leg: all he has to do is give the aids for the opposite canter. However, he should never attempt to 'throw' the horse onto the opposite leg by swinging his upper body from one side to the other. This is incorrect and usually leads to the horse changing only in front or behind, or simply continuing on the same lead.

If the horse and rider do have problems with the flying changes, the change of leg should be made through trot for the time being. A smooth transition through trot is preferable to a forced flying change, which simply creates tension in the horse.

Riding courses should not be something which is done only in competitions. Not until complete courses can be jumped reliably in a training situation should the rider consider jumping in competitions.

At this point it is worth repeating yet again that the novice rider should not be overfaced. The aim of jumping training is not to jump higher and higher fences, but rather to teach the rider to:

* maintain an active canter, suitable to jump from
* keep a rhythm
* make the approach to the centre of the fence
* make the correct approach for the fence
* land straight and continue smoothly and harmoniously to the next fence, taking the correct number of strides.

Plan for performing and training the basic jumping exercises

* Walk on a loose or long rein.
* Loosening exercises (to obtain and develop *Losgelassenheit),* in trot and canter, on straight and curved tracks.

To improve the rider's suppleness and balance in the light seat:
* position/seat training and exercises
* riding transitions from one gait to another, and within a gait, with shortened stirrups
* work over cavalletti, in walk, trot and canter.

Depending on the level and purpose of the training the next stages may be as follows:
* jumping single fences from trot and canter, with or without a placing pole
* gradually adding more jumps to form a grid
* jumping combinations
* riding related distances on straight and curved tracks

* varying the number of strides between fences
* jumping different kinds of fences
* riding several jumps in succession and sections of courses.

* Relaxation and cooling down.

3.4 Basic Exercises in Outdoor and Cross-Country Riding and Jumping

Riding outdoors and across country are an important part of the basic training. They offer a particularly educational experience because they contain so many natural challenges. They improve the rider's skill and suppleness, as well as helping to promote looseness (*Losgelassenheit*) in the horse and to build its confidence.

Riding out in a rural setting is a stimulating and refreshing experience for rider and horse and is a reward for all the hard work done in the school. Hence it also serves to create **enthusiasm** and **motivation** for future training.

The rider should be given the opportunity to ride out regularly and his cross-country training should run parallel to his dressage and jumping training. He should be taught, on a step-by-step basis, to control the horse out of doors, to ride over different kinds of terrain and in different going and to jump natural obstacles. Regular, systematic training across country will enable the rider to cope confidently with hacking out, trekking, hunting and horse trials.

NOTE   A true horseman can handle his horse in any setting or surroundings.

For basic training, it is essential that suitable horses are available for cross-country work, as well as for dressage and jumping. Safety considerations and suitable tack are discussed in Section 3.3.

Riding outdoors should begin early in the rider's training. The essential prerequisite is a **secure seat** in both the dressage and the jumping position.

The seat should be sufficiently established for the rider to be able to remain in the saddle even when something unexpected happens. In cross-country riding the rider's balance is particularly important because he needs to be constantly adapting, in movement, to the changes in the horse's balance.

Riding out in walk, perhaps with periods in trot, can be introduced even earlier in the training, provided particularly quiet horses are used. It is for the instructor to decide whether it is feasible to do so.

Preparation for outdoor and cross-country work consists in working in the three basic gaits in a large **outdoor arena.** The rider can then practise controlling the pace and length of stride. He must be able to keep the horse well 'on the aids' and be in a position to use his driving and restraining aids at all times. In keeping with the longer frame in which the horse is working, the rider's hands should be carried lower, and he should 'give' elastically from his shoulders and elbows to allow the horse to stretch its neck as required. As in the other forms of riding, a steady, soft contact should be maintained.

As the rider becomes more secure, work on varied types of **natural terrain** and gentle **slopes** can be introduced. As far as possible an even rhythm and steady pace should be maintained. Since riding over this type of ground means that the horse's balance is constantly changing, the rider needs to learn to adapt his centre of gravity to that of the horse. Hence this work will also improve and confirm the rider's skill in riding in the light seat and in varying the amount of weight on the horse's back.

Once the rider's balance is established, he can ride up and down gentle slopes and across **undulating terrain** (a combination of gentle up-and-down slopes) at a canter, making sure that the rhythm is maintained.

Riding up- and downhill

When riding **up- and downhill** the rider leans forward, taking the weight off the horse's back. When riding uphill, the steeper the slope, the more the rider needs to lean forward. When riding down a steep slope, the rider adopts a less forward position but still keeps the weight off the horse's back. If the rider is still a bit unsteady, a neckstrap can be used or the reins formed into a bridge on the horse's neck to give extra support. Riding downhill in particular requires a well-developed sense of balance.

At a more advanced stage of training, steep up and down slopes can be introduced. These must always be ridden straight, i.e. not obliquely. For steep slopes, a firm seat is needed: the knees should be against the horse, with the lower legs next to the girth, and the heels flexed downwards and forwards. This is the only way the rider can remain in balance and avoid using the reins for support.

Cantering up- and downhill should only be done if the slope and the going are suitable. The horse should remain well 'on the aids' and the rhythm should be maintained.

Riding on different surfaces and through water

Depending on the type of going and the situation, certain safety and practical considerations should be borne in mind. On **deep or marshy ground**, the rider should take the weight off the horse's back and hindquarters. He should press his knees firmly against the horse, incline his upper body forward and give the horse as much rein as necessary. If the horse sinks excessively, the rider should jump down and lead it, giving it plenty of rein.

Tarmac roads should be crossed only in walk or at a slow trot and in a straight line.

On **slippery or icy surfaces,** the rider should dismount and lead the horse. To

Riding across undulating terrain

prevent the horse slipping, only gentle turns should be made.

At first, when **riding through water,** crossing places should be chosen where the bottom is level and firm underfoot and the water shallow. The horse should be able to feel the ground under its feet at all times. The first few times, an experienced rider on a suitable horse should take the lead in order to give the other riders confidence.

Particularly in shallow water, the riders should make sure that their horses do not roll. A hot, sweaty horse with no fear of water will often indicate its intention to do so by stopping and pawing with its forefeet. The rider should immediately shorten the reins and ride energetically forward.

Once the horse has gone through the water a few times in walk, if the location is suitable, it can then be ridden through at a steady trot and later in canter.

If there is a **steep bank** leading into the water, the horse should jump down into the water calmly, with the rider in the same position as for riding downhill. The weight should also be taken off the horse's back when riding through **deep water.** It is particularly important that the rider's knees are pressed firmly against the horse with the lower legs next to the girth. The rider should allow the horse enough rein to stretch its head and neck as required.

Rhythm and pace

In the next phase of cross-country training, the rider needs to be taught to develop a feel for rhythm and pace. This is important both for going out on rides and for competing in show jumping and cross-country events. It also prevents him from pushing the horse too hard through ignorance.

The rider should be asked to ride a track of specified length, preferably with intermediate distances markers to allow him to judge his pace, i.e. his speed. The first priority is to ensure that the rhythm and pace remain constant. This is essential to prevent undue strain on the horse when being ridden for long distances. It allows the horse to perform much more efficiently.

The next step is to maintain a set pace and so a set speed. **Normal speeds** are as follows:

Walk: approx. 100-125m per minute.
Working trot: approx. 220-250m per minute.
Working canter: approx. 330-400m per minute.
(This means that 1km in walk takes about 8-10 minutes, in trot 4-5 minutes, and in canter 2.5-3 minutes.)

The rider should use the distance markers and a watch to help him learn the feel of a normal-speed walk, trot and canter. Variations of pace and speed in each gait, especially canter, can be practised in subsequent lessons.

In novice horse trials in Germany, a speed of 500m per minute is required in the cross-country phase. [Note: In other countries, the speed requirement may be different.]

Cross-country obstacles

Once the horse and rider can jump cavalletti and small fences consistently in the school, training in **jumping natural obstacles** can begin. Small obstacles should be chosen to start with, for example logs, small stone walls and narrow ditches. These can also be used to prepare for and complement the jumping

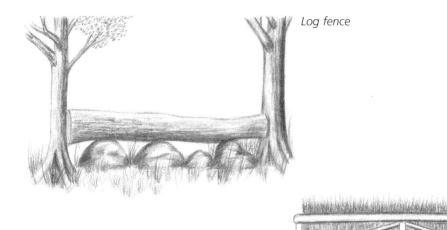

Log fence

Portable cross-country fence

exercises done in the school. On no account should the obstacles be bigger than the fences the horse has so far been used to jumping in the school.

People tend to be wary of solid obstacles, such as occur naturally in the countryside. However, fixed cross-country fences and obstacles are preferable by far to the knock-down type since they require the horse to be more careful and are therefore less dangerous.

The cross-country obstacles used in the rider's early training should be closed in at the side to prevent the horse running out (for example, they should be built into an existing hedge or across a sunken track or a woodland path).

Portable cross-country obstacles have also been found to be practical and effective in many situations but they must be stable, solidly built and imposing.

At a more advanced level of training, rails, banks, troughs, walls and ditches can be used and combined to make varied, interesting and 'educational' obstacles.

When riding an **approach** to a cross-country obstacle, the same applies as when jumping in the school, i.e. it should

be approached straight and at a suitable pace. The obstacle should be jumped a few times out of trot and then from canter. The rider should keep the horse in front of his legs and his driving aids in order to maintain the rhythm and balance. The strides should not be lengthened or shortened excessively.

The rider should never be complacent about even the simplest of jumps, or ride at it in a 'happy-go-lucky' fashion. This puts the horse off and increases the risk of a refusal. The rider must have made up his mind to do the jump but this does not mean that he should increase the pace and force the horse at the fence. He should maintain the rhythm and allow the horse to find the take-off point more or less by itself out of this rhythm. An experienced cross-country horse should be able to 'help itself' where necessary, and judge the take-off point in accordance with the type and size of the obstacle. This will enable it to find its own way out of difficult situations.

When jumping onto **banks and steps** the rider should incline his body further forward and allow the horse more rein. The horse will describe a steeper path through the air. The rider's knees should be firmly against the saddle and his lower legs just behind the girth. This sort of obstacle is approached on a longer stride, and with increased impulsion, but the horse must remain on the aids at all times, and not 'fall apart'.

Drop fences are approached on a shorter stride. To decrease the canter strides, the rider should 'sit down' a little more while still keeping the horse in front of the driving aids.

Drop fences without a pole or obstacle on top can also be jumped from trot (sitting) or even from a walk.

When jumping any drop fence, in order to avoid disturbing the horse in its back as it lands it is important to maintain a steady contact, to keep the knees firmly against the saddle and to accompany the movement smoothly. Pushing the heels forward and down will help the rider to keep his balance during the landing.

Ditches are commonly found natural obstacles. Small dry ditches should be chosen to begin with in order to build the rider's confidence. They should be approached calmly, first in trot and later in canter. The rider should send the horse

forward with positive driving aids used in conjunction with an 'allowing' hand.

For a seasoned cross-country horse, jumping ditches usually presents no problems. However, even an experienced horse may sometimes stop for a look. This is not an immediate cause for concern or for punishing the horse. What will probably happen, especially if the lead horse is already on the other side, is that the horse will take off suddenly after it has had a look at the ditch. The rider should be prepared for this and should take hold of the neckstrap if necessary to avoid catching the horse in the mouth during the jump.

As in dressage and show jumping training, the rider should never lose patience: he should continue to ride the horse calmly using the correct aids.

When **jumping into water** the water has a braking effect. The rider should allow the horse enough rein for it to be able to adjust its balance accordingly. He should continue to lean forward during the landing phase, and should counteract the loss of momentum by pressing his knees firmly into the saddle and pushing his heels forward and down. If he

Bank or step obstacle

straightens up too soon during the jump he will no longer be in balance with the horse. If problems arise during the jump, a fall is then more likely to result than if the rider is in harmony with the horse's movement.

Basic cross-country training should always be carried out under the supervision of an experienced trainer or instructor. He is the best person to judge the right demands to make on horse and rider.

Cross-country obstacles

Rails

Pheasant-feeder type fence

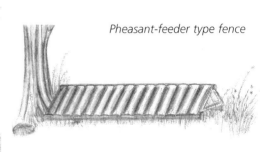

Palisade

Trakehner

Wood pile

Straw bales

NOTE   The aim of basic cross-country training is to teach the rider to find his way smoothly, systematically and safely over whatever lies in his path. It should not consist of the rider jumping fences haphazardly and constantly having to pluck up his courage to do so.

Plan for performing and training exercises in cross-country riding and jumping

* Walk on a loose or long rein.

* Exercises to develop looseness (*Losgelassenheit*) on straight and curved tracks.

* Exercises to improve the rider's suppleness and balance in the light seat:
  – working trot, rising, with shortened stirrups
  – working canter, using the light seat
  – riding at different, specified speeds (variations of pace within a gait), and controlled riding of turns.

Depending on the level and the purpose of the training, the following can be introduced progressively:
* riding on different kinds of surface
* riding on natural and undulating terrain
* riding up- and downhill
* riding a specified distance at a specified speed, with distance markers along the route so that the rider can judge and develop a feel for the pace
* jumping low natural obstacles
* jumping natural obstacles on sloping ground
* jumping ditches
* jumping onto and off banks, over drop fences, and into water.

* Relaxation and cooling-down phase.

3.5 Weekend and Long-Distance Rides

Rides which take place over a period of several days need to be thoroughly planned beforehand. Weekend rides will normally be within a 50km (31 mile) radius of home. Long-distance rides extend over longer periods and cover greater distances.

Both horse and rider need to be prepared for these rides. Special events such as this require systematic planning and training. The rider needs to be physically fit, for example. This is achieved through regular long sessions in the saddle, including lengthy periods in trot. A tired rider weighs more heavily on the horse's back.

Taking the weight off the horse's back temporarily increases its performance considerably and so the rider must be able to get off and walk for considerable distances. Dismounting and leading the horse gives the rider a break as well as the horse. Since going up hills is much more strenuous than travelling on level ground, it is much easier for the horse if the rider dismounts on steep hills. It is also a good idea to lead the horse on long downhill stretches.

Tack also requires special attention, the more so since when riding long distances there is usually some luggage which needs to be attached to the saddle. The rider should experiment beforehand to find the best way of packing the bags and attaching the various items to the saddle.

During the run-up to the ride, the horse's health and fitness should be monitored by checking and recording its heart rate, respiration and temperature. The feet and shoes should be in good condition. Horses with bad feet should not be used for long-distance rides. If the horse needs to be re-shod, this should be done at least eight days before the beginning of the ride.

Planning the ride properly and dividing it up into sections of suitable length is essential. A short distance ridden thoughtlessly can take more out of rider and horse than a longer leg on which attention has been paid to pace, speed and rest periods.

The best way to travel is in twos. The rules of the road must be strictly adhered to. In poor light, the group should carry white lights at the front and red lights at the back.

Food for horse and rider should be based on the energy output. Frequent small meals are more suitable than larger quantities provided at more widely spaced intervals.

> **NOTE** The best foundation for rides requiring stamina and endurance is good instruction, and fitness in horse and rider.

3.6 Hunting, Drag Hunts and Simulated Hunts

Hunting and simulated hunting is an enjoyable and at the same time very educational experience. It requires forward riding over unfamiliar terrain, stamina, boldness and a good 'rapport' between horse and rider. The aim is not to win prizes but simply to enjoy riding over country at speed in the company of other horses and riders.

In the autumn, every riding school and club should organise some simulated hunts. However, only riders and horses who have undergone systematic preparation should take part. Training should be carried out by a suitably experienced person, and some suitable wide, solid, natural obstacles should be available for practice.

The riders can be divided up into different groups, or 'fields', according to their level of experience. Work at a fast, hunting pace should be incorporated, but most of the work should be at a moderate pace in order to avoid placing excessive strain on the horses.

Riding behind a pack of hounds, with the hounds setting the pace, is not possible in most riding clubs and schools. Usually, therefore, one rider goes out in front to lead the way and set the pace, and the rest of the field follows behind the 'master'. On no account should any member of the field overtake the master. Each rider should look ahead and decide on a line to ride and maintain pace and rhythm. He should avoid crossing in front of other riders and should keep his distance from other horses when jumping (this is why the jumps need to be wide).

The rider should keep the same position for the duration of the hunt and never gallop up to other horses from behind and overtake them. He should keep his distance from the horse in front in case it or its rider falls. Horses which are excitable or not reliable jumpers should be ridden on the outside of the group. If the rider loses control, he should leave by turning away from the field to the outside. If his horse refuses, the rider should act immediately to ensure that he does not get in the way of other riders. In the event of a fall, the rider should try to fall sideways and perform a roll over his shoulder while still keeping hold of the reins. Holding onto the horse will prevent it running loose and endangering the other riders, and also enables the rider to remount and continue.

Of course, the rider should also show consideration towards his horse, ensuring that it is not sweating when it arrives at the 'meet', checking the tack at intervals, leading it round at the end to cool it off if necessary, riding considerately on the way home and looking after it properly on arrival.

Cherished hunting traditions, which have survived over centuries, should be preserved and kept alive wherever possible.

4 THE BASIC TRAINING OF THE HORSE

The aim of the basic training is to produce a horse which goes kindly, is obedient, willing and able to use itself. Through familiarisation, careful training and suppling, or 'gymnasticising', the horse's natural aptitudes are preserved and developed, and placed at the rider's disposal for use in the appropriate situations. Flatwork, i.e. basic dressage, forms the basis of this training. It is an essential prerequisite for all further training in any discipline.

In contrast to the earlier part of the book, in this section it is assumed that the rider can sit, ride and apply the aids to the necessary standard, and has the necessary 'feel'. A young horse should always be ridden by an experienced rider who will be able to ascertain its strengths and weaknesses and adapt the training accordingly. Rigid training regimes which disregard the horse's individual characteristics are simply half-measures which result in tense, resistant horses which are difficult and unpleasant to ride and are a lasting source of dissatisfaction for all concerned.

> **NOTE** A young horse should always be ridden by an experienced rider.

Training under saddle should not begin until the end of the horse's third year. It should be stepped up **gradually,** according to the horse's build, constitution and development.

Once the horse has been backed, at least a year should be allowed for training to novice competition level. This should be an **all-round training** which will also enable the horse to go on to specialise in one discipline if required. **Specialising too early** is a bad thing because it results in an unbalanced education which is lacking in variety. A horse which has not received an all-round basic training will be less supple and able to use itself, and less 'through' (Durchlässigkeit).

If used correctly, a horse will usually be able to continue taking part in competitions until it is fifteen to eighteen years old. The fact that it has been kept fit and supple will then often enable it be used for several more years for hacking or as a schoolmaster for young riders.

4.1 The Rider

To understand and train young horses properly, many years experience of riding many different horses is required. To be able to give the horse its basic dressage, show jumping and cross-country training, the rider himself needs to have received an **all-round training.** Specialising too early, even if the horse seems to have exceptional ability in one area, is contrary to the principles of classical horsemanship, and the trainer also runs the risk of overfacing and souring the horse.

The trainer needs a great deal of

sensitivity and experience to be able to judge how best to proceed in each individual case. Undergoing further training and listening to the viewpoints of other experienced riders will provide the trainer with useful guidelines by which to judge his horse's progress.

In horse training, as in rider training, the trainer needs to adhere to certain proven **principles:**

* the training should be based on a plan
* it should be systematic and progressive
* the method should be correct
* the training should have continuity
* it should be a varied, comprehensive, all-round training
* there should be adequate breaks and relaxation periods
* the training should be clear and consistent
* the rider should not allow uncontrolled emotions to play any part in his training
* progress should be assessed regularly
* the individual characteristics of the horse should be taken into account
* the training should result in a physically and mentally well-balanced horse and rider.

As any good trainer and rider with 'horse sense' will understand, correct basic training results in a horse which is contented and uninhibited. In training and riding, the horse's **mental well-being** is important and forms the basis for a harmonious rapport between horse and rider.

4.2 The Horse's Development and Behaviour

A horse is usually fully grown by the time it is four or five years old. At the age of three to three and a half, it can be backed over a period of a few weeks then turned away for a several months to mature. Training can then recommence at three and a half to four years of age.

In order to avoid overtaxing and harming the horse physically and mentally, the rider needs to have, as well as the necessary riding skills, a basic understanding of animal psychology. Horses are easily upset by incorrect riding, and it can take months, or often even years, to rectify the damage. Bad training can also lead to premature wear and injury, especially to the limbs.

The following **psychological guidelines** may be useful:

* physically and by nature, the horse is a highly specialised creature of flight; it is also a herd animal and feels safest when surrounded by its fellows

* the horse sees man as one of its fellows; as the horse's teacher, man needs to take the place of a horse higher in the hierarchy or 'pecking order'

* this is achieved through understanding and not by force – when the horse makes mistakes, i.e. does not respond as required to the trainer's instructions, this is only because it has not understood correctly

* to be able to understand the trainer, the horse needs to **trust** him – understanding is based on trust

* man, i.e. the trainer, communicates with the horse through the aids and the auxiliary aids, i.e. the voice, touch, weight and reward

* the horse will only understand the rider's

instructions properly if it understands the aids; the horse's primitive, instinctive reaction is to run away from strange or unknown objects and situations and so the horse needs to be acquainted with them gradually and systematically – if fear or uncertainty arise, the trainer should go back and start again; he should also bear in mind that the horse has an excellent **memory** – it remembers the good things and the bad things which happen to it, and it can take a long time for it to forget a bad experience

* the horse's ability to learn depends on it being sufficiently mature physically – making excessive physical or mental demands will cause setbacks in the horse's training

* the horse will achieve its full potential only if its needs are fulfilled and if it is in harmony with its environment – of which man is a part

* the horse must associate man with **security,** in every situation.

The trainer must also understand the role of the horse's **senses.**

Smell is the most highly developed of the horse's senses although it is not of much help in training. It does, however, exercise a negative influence at times, for example, when the horse reacts to smell it does not like (e.g. a pig farm) or which brings back unpleasant memories (smoke or the smell of chemicals or drugs).

The horse's **hearing** is also highly developed. It is for this reason that unnecessary loud noises should be avoided in the stable and during training.

The horse's **sight** is not very well developed. However, owing to the position of the eyes on the side of the head, the horse has a much wider field of vision than man, i.e. than its rider.

The horse has an exceptional ability to perceive movement, particularly to the side and in the distance. It will see something moving sooner and more clearly than its rider does so that the rider often has no idea why the horse has suddenly shied.

The horse's sense of **touch** and its **sensitivity to touch** are highly developed. It is this sensitivity which allows the rider to fine-tune his aids.

Observing the horse's eyes, ears, tail and breathing, and watching the skin for signs of sweating, will give the trainer an insight into the horse's mental state.

The **eyes** reflect the horse's state of mind. They can express attentiveness, confidence, mistrust or fear. The **ear movements** can also provide important information about the horse's emotional state. Laid-back or flattened ears always indicate that the horse is ill at ease and ready to defend itself. Mobile or pricked ears denote attentiveness and a willing attitude.

Snorting or 'sneezing', in conjunction with a swinging, freely carried **tail** indicate that the horse is free from tension, and is working or ready to work.

A tail which is tensed, clamped down or carried high is a sign of fear, tension or excitement.

Sweating can be caused not only by exertion but by excitement. It is usually accompanied by raised heart and respiration rates.

The most important qualities required in a trainer are understanding, sensitivity, calmness and consistency. Nervous, highly strung people are also usually impatient and do not have the necessary calm, objective approach.

Conscientious repetition of practices necessary for safe handling of the horse, such as tying it up, lifting up the feet, leading and making it stand, will help to establish a habit of obedience in the horse. Rewarding, scolding, and the appropriate punishment where necessary, should be related directly to what has happened, or what it is hoped to achieve. Constantly feeding the horse sugar, carrots or other titbits for no particular reason will spoil it and eventually lead it to try to place itself above the trainer in the 'pecking order'. Unreasonable or excessive punishment, on the other hand, will lead to resistance, and may eventually make the horse vicious and dangerous.

In training horses, it is a big mistake to expect the horse's reactions to be based on thought processes similar to those of a human. Horses, like all animals, will always act in accordance with primitive, inherited reflexes.

The rider's weight brings about changes in the horse's **natural balance,** and these changes need to be taken into account in the horse's training and development.

The horse's body forms the basis for its movement, its action and its performance under the rider. The proportions of the body and limbs, and the associated musculature, have a decisive influence on the movement.

Good conformation, combined with good action, a good temperament and systematic schooling, or 'gymnasticising', provide the best foundations for developing balance and self-carriage under the rider.

At first, the weight of the rider disturbs the young horse's balance. The rider should aim to re-establish this balance during the early stages of training by use of his weight, legs and hands. He needs to make it possible for the horse to balance itself, without constraint, and while maintaining its natural forward movement.

NOTE   The rider must remember that the horse's balance will be affected at first by the weight of the rider on its back.

It is the trainer's responsibility to use his knowledge, combined with patience and constant observation, to get the horse to cooperate willingly. The musculature needs to be gradually developed to enable the horse to regain its natural balance and then, later, to allow more weight to be transferred onto the hindquarters.

Only through progressive, systematic training can the horse recover under the rider its natural balance in the three basic gaits and on slopes.

4.3 The Basic Gaits

One important function of basic training is to preserve and refine the purity and regularity of the natural gaits. It is therefore essential that the trainer knows exactly how the horse moves in each of the three basic gaits, because only then will he be in a position to take the appropriate action to correct or improve them.

NOTE   The rhythm must be maintained in each of the basic gaits, and in each form of the gait, i.e. working, collected and extended, etc.

Walk

The walk is a marching movement in which the feet are set down one after the other in four-time, with no moment of suspension (suspension phase). The walk consists of eight phases, with the horse being supported alternately by two, then three legs. Hence the feet are moved forward in an alternating diagonal/lateral sequence, for example, right fore, left hind, left fore, right hind (see opposite). The easiest way to check that the footfalls are in four-time and evenly spaced is to listen to the hoof beats on a hard surface. When seen from the ground, the foreleg and hind leg on the same side should on no account look parallel, or nearly parallel. In fact they should form a 'V' shape for a brief moment, with the hind foot, as it swings forward, almost touching the forefoot. If the feet on the same side are moved forward and set down simultaneously, the horse is performing an incorrect gait known as 'pacing'.

The different forms of walk are:

The **medium walk,** in which the hind feet are set down in front of the prints of the forefeet. The horse walks forward with a steady, soft contact. The rider 'allows' the natural movement of the horse's head in time with the walk. The medium walk is the horse's natural walk.

In the **collected walk,** the hind feet at set down no further forward than the prints of the forefeet. The horse is higher in front, and shorter, i.e. he is more 'upright', as a result of, and in keeping with the collection and the increased flexion of the hindquarters or 'haunches'. The activity of the walk is maintained. The nose is nearly vertical. The steps are more expressive.

In the **extended walk** the horse takes long, ground covering steps. The stride length depends on the horse's natural aptitude and conformation, but it must be seen to be longer than in medium walk.

Trot

The trot is a two time movement consisting of four phases. The legs are picked up, carried forward and set down in diagonal pairs. Since one diagonal pair is picked up before the other is set down, there is a moment of suspension in between (see opposite). The following forms of trot are recognised:

The **working trot** is the form most frequently used in basic training, and for this reason it merits special attention. The working trot must always be active. The horse should work with 'looseness' *(Losgelassenheit)* and take regular, ground-covering, active steps (i.e. it should work energetically from behind). The hind feet should be set down approximately in the prints of the forefeet.

In the **medium trot,** the horse covers more ground by lengthening, and not quickening, its strides. The powerful thrust of the hind feet enables the forefeet to be raised and carried lightly and freely. The hind feet are set down in front of the prints of the forefeet.

The neck is stretched slightly, bringing the nose a little further in front of the vertical, i.e. the frame is lengthened. The horse should continue to yield through its poll and should remain in self-carriage.

Lengthening the strides in trot is a preliminary to medium trot. Medium trot should be developed gradually out of the working trot, and the lengthened strides should be seen as part of this progression.

In the **collected trot** there is increased flexion of the hindquarter joints (haunches) and the hind legs engage further underneath the horse's body in the direction of the centre of gravity. Hence the steps cover less ground, but the energy, activity and impulsion are maintained. The horse carries less weight on its forehand, and becomes higher in front and shorter in its body (more 'upright'). The steps are also higher. The

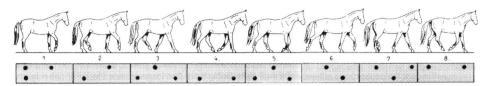

Walk

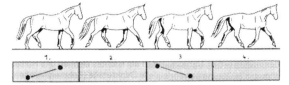

Trot

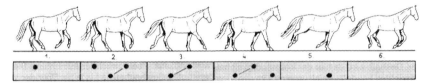

Right canter

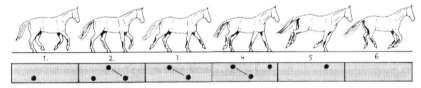

Left canter

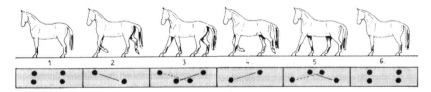

Rein-back

hind feet are set down no further forward than the prints of the forefeet.

The **extended trot** is the most ground-covering trot. The horse should show as much impulsion and forward thrust as possible, and cover as much ground as possible, and at the same time should also lengthen its frame accordingly. The rider should get the horse to lengthen its frame by allowing it to take the rein forward more and stretch its neck. The hind feet should be set down well in front of the prints of the forefeet.

Only if the horse can be collected, and so take more of its weight on its hindquarters, will it be able to perform the extended trot without falling onto its forehand.

Canter

The canter is a three-time gait, consisting of a series of jump-like movements, in between which there is a moment of suspension. The canter may be 'on the left leg' (left canter) or 'on the right leg' (right canter) depending on which pair of legs steps further forward. The sequence is as follows: first the outside hind leg, then the inside hind leg and the outside foreleg together, followed by the inside foreleg, and finally the moment of suspension (suspension phase). Hence the left canter, for example, is made up of the following phases (see also page 129):

* right hind foot on the ground (one-point base of support),
* right hind, left hind and right fore on the ground together (three-point base of support),
* left hind and right fore (diagonal pair) on the ground (two-point base of support),
* left hind and right fore, plus left fore (three-point base of support again),
* left fore only on the ground (one-point base of support again),
* moment of suspension.

The different forms of canter are as follows:

The **working canter,** which should be active and regular, full of impulsion, and in clearly defined three-time. Each stride should cover a distance approximately equal to a horse's length.

In the **medium canter,** longer, more ground-covering strides are required, in conjunction with a more extended frame.

Lengthening the strides in canter is a preliminary to medium canter. The length of the strides should be increased to give a gradual progression from working to medium canter.

In the **collected canter,** the hind legs engage further under the body without losing their activity and take more of the weight. As a result, the horse takes higher steps.

In the **extended canter** the horse covers as much ground as possible. It must extend its frame accordingly while at the same time remaining on the contact. The strides should be longer but not quicker than in the medium canter. As in the extended trot, collection is an essential prerequisite.

Rein-back

Although not one of the basic paces, the rein-back also has a designated sequence of footfalls and is included here in order to complete the picture. The rein-back is a two-time movement in which the feet are picked up, moved back and set down in diagonal pairs. One diagonal pair of feet is set down before the other is picked up so that there is no moment of suspension.

Specialised gaits

The basic gaits of the riding horse are walk, trot and canter. Inherited or acquired paces are the 'tölt' and the 'pace'.

The **tölt** is a movement in rapid four-time with the head carried relatively high. The speed should be at least 200m per minute. In spite of the energetic forward movement and the high action, the tölt is easy to sit to since the steps are quick and follow in rapid succession and do not throw the rider out of the saddle.

In the **pace** the legs are raised, swung forward and set down in lateral pairs. Since it is not a bouncy gait, it is not tiring for the rider, which may appeal in cases where travelling and covering long distances are involved. In most cases, pacing is a trained movement, i.e. an acquired gait.

4.4 Initial Handling and Backing

Handling in the stable

In most cases, the horse's basic training takes place in a different environment from that in which it grew up. Settling in, and getting used to its **new surroundings, stabling and diet** is crucial to the horse's future development. The trainer must be prepared to use tact and patience, and give it the necessary time to adjust. Usually a few days will suffice but in some cases several weeks may be required.

During the period when the horse is being backed, turning it out more in the field or exercise area will help to work off excess energy and tension and to keep it happy and well-adjusted.

Particular care should be taken over the first stage of training, which consists of familiarising the horse with the **saddle and bridle.** It is best to introduce it to these in the familiar surroundings of its stable. The pleasant associations of the stable, i.e. food and comfort, will help it to accept the unfamiliar equipment.

First the bridle is put on. It is a good idea to attach a lunge line to the bridle to ensure that the trainer keeps control if the horse tries to pull away. If it manages to escape when the saddle and bridle are being put on for the first time, it often takes a long time to get it to accept them calmly.

To start with, many horses dislike the girth being tightened, and the saddle should be put on for the first time in the school, for example, where there is a soft surface, or at least in a yard where there is plenty of room. An elasticated girth will help to avoid creating unnecessary tension. Even if the horse knows the handlers, and has been familiarised with the saddle, it is almost inevitable that it will give a few bucks to try to get rid of it and this could lead to falls and serious injury if it is in the stable or, even worse, in the stable corridor at the time.

The trainer should always work with an assistant – never alone. A quiet manner and a reassuring voice are important. Food can be used as a reward during training.

Lungeing

Lungeing is an effective, and in many cases essential preparation for ridden training. The aim of lungeing is:
* to get the horse used to working
* to teach it obedience
* to develop rhythm and looseness (*Losgelassenheit*).

Lungeing is also useful in later training as a means of correcting faults in the horse's position and gaits which have developed under saddle. It is also beneficial for horses with conformation defects, and for improving problem areas such as the neck and back. Other uses are for giving light exercise to horses which have been ill, or simply to provide variety in the training.

When teaching the young horse to lunge, the lunger should be accompanied by an assistant. The lunger stands in the centre while the assistant leads the horse out onto the circle, then walks around next to its head. Once the lunger and the helper feel that the horse will stay on the circle of its own accord, the assistant can walk back to the lunger, take the whip, and then walk along level with the horse's hind legs.

When getting the horse used to being lunged, it is important that the trainer keeps perfectly calm and makes his intentions absolutely clear. Provided these conditions are met, the horse will quickly learn to respond to the lunge, whip and voice aids and will soon be lungeing freely on both reins.

To begin with, side-reins should either not be fitted or should be fitted loosely, and the horse should therefore be lunged in a special lunge ring or in a confined area. As a rule, the trainer can start to use side-reins (single side-reins or double 'running' reins) after about three or four days. Their height should be such that when the horse flexes correctly, its mouth is approximately level with its shoulder joint. The nose should be about 10cm in front of the vertical – never behind it.

The side-reins should be of equal length so as not to interfere with the horse's natural balance, and not to encourage crookedness. When the horse starts to lower its head and seek the contact, it must be allowed to do so. The lunge rein can be used to obtain a flexion to the inside.

The correct length and height of the side-reins should be determined through experience and observation. The aim is for the horse to 'go into' them and seek a contact.

Particularly in the early stages, the horse should be lunged for no more than 20-30 minutes. There should be frequent changes of rein and the horse should be given plenty of praise.

Further guidelines on lungeing young, and older, horses are contained in Book 6: *Lungeing*, also in this series.

Backing and preliminary work under saddle

The horse is prepared for backing as part of its daily care and handling. It gets used to feeling the groom or handler run his hand over its back, pat it all over or lean carefully across his withers.

Even the quietest, most phlegmatic horse will sometimes take fright and react violently if the rider suddenly sits on its back with no warning, and so backing the horse should always be carried out very carefully, in a quiet, relaxed manner, and the trainer must be prepared to take his time. Choosing the right rider can be crucial. He or she should be experienced and knowledgeable, neither nervous nor too heavy, and have a good, balanced seat. Situations may arise which could otherwise be dangerous for the rider and at the same time cause the horse to lose confidence. The success or otherwise of this experience will be crucial to the horse's future progress.

The horse should be mounted for the first time on the lunge, in an enclosed arena or, better still, in an indoor school. One person should hold the horse while another carefully legs up the rider. With nervous horses it is sometimes a good idea to lie across the saddle first. The rider should then slide smoothly into the saddle, without touching the horse's croup (this in itself requires a certain skill). The stirrups should be slightly shorter than normal so as to avoid putting too much weight on the horse's back.

Being patted, praised and fed sugar by someone it knows and trusts will help to take the horse's mind off the new experience. The rider can hold on to a neck strap or the mane in case the horse bucks. On no account should he hold on by the reins.

The person holding the lunge then carefully tries to lead the horse forward, and talks reassuringly to it. When the horse starts to move, the rider follows the movement elastically but passively. Frequent halts and patting help to put the horse at ease.

When the horse starts to move forward more confidently under the rider's weight, the lunge can be gradually lengthened until the horse is on the normal circle used for lungeing.

These early exercises should be fairly short. The horse should learn to accept the rider's weight calmly, at first in walk, and then in trot. At the end of the lesson, the rider can practise dismounting and mounting again a few times, perhaps using the stirrup to mount if all goes well.

For lungeing and backing, particular emphasis should be laid on correctly fitting saddlery and equipment. Young horses are often relatively 'shapeless' and do not muscle up and develop a more distinct shape until later in their training. The rider should therefore remove and replace the saddle at regular intervals – usually it is not enough simply to keep on tightening the girths. Getting off the horse to reposition the saddle also serves to give its back a short rest.

The next stage in the training under saddle is easier if the young horse can be ridden in the company of other horses. Using one or more **lead horses** seems to be the best system. If only one lead horse is available, it should be positioned alongside and slightly in front of the young horse. With two lead horses, one should be placed immediately in front of the young horse, and the other alongside and level with it. An outer wall or fence is also important. The young horse then has no escape route and will quickly and willingly adapt to the gait and length of stride of

the 'herd', and allow itself to be steered in the same direction. All that the horse needs to learn at this stage is to go freely forwards in its natural **walk and trot.**

The rider should not wear spurs but should carry a short, flexible (but not too flexible) whip. The whip and the voice are used to help teach the horse to respond to the forward-driving leg aids.

> **NOTE**   One of the main objectives in training is to preserve or create in the horse the desire for active forward movement.

Sending the horse forward a bit too freely is preferable to trying to shorten its natural way of going. The reins should be long enough to prevent unintentional interference with the mouth.

Only if the rider concentrates on **riding forwards,** rather than 'placing' the horse's head with his hands, will he be laying the foundations for correct training.

However, riding the horse forwards should not degenerate into pushing it out of a rhythm and causing it to hurry. The pace and length of stride should be suited to the horse.

If the horse breaks spontaneously into a **canter,** it should be allowed to continue. The rider should ease the weight on the horse's back to allow it maximum freedom. It should not be allowed to canter for long periods to start with, since its balance will not be sufficiently established.

Rest periods in the lesson can be used to further develop the horse's obedience and confidence. For example, the rider can practise **halting,** although without too much attention to the direction the horse faces or how it stands. Standing calmly while the rider repositions the saddle is also good practice.

To sum up, when backing horses the

following points should be borne in mind:

* Young horses should only be ridden by experienced lightweight riders, particularly in the initial stages, until the back muscles become stronger.

* Bumps or jarring movements on the horse's back cause tension and every attempt should be made to avoid them. The rider should therefore take care when mounting, sit softly into the movements and ride with a moderately light seat and shortish stirrups.

* The horse should learn to move under saddle with its natural, rhythmic, springy, ground-covering action. This is only possible if its back muscles are free from tension. Tension is created by the rider sitting on the horse's back, and must be counteracted by exercises aimed at developing looseness *(Losgelassenheit)* and calmness.

* As the horse relaxes, in a loose rein walk to start with, it will stretch its head and neck forwards and downwards, its back and tail will start to swing and it will take rhythmic, ground-covering steps with his hind legs engaging well underneath its body. Only when this stage has been reached should the rider start to work on

the horse's position and carriage by riding it forward onto a light contact in trot, canter, and finally in walk.

Loose jumping

Loose jumping can be included in the horse's early education alongside its backing and familiarisation training. It adds variety to the training, and at the same time helps to develop the horse's agility and suppleness. It also makes the subsequent jumping training easier.

The young horse should be loose-jumped approximately once a week. In order to prevent accidents and loss of confidence, certain procedures should be adhered to, and precautions taken:

* For loose jumping, the horse should be fitted with bandages or boots on the forelegs and possibly also the hind legs. Over-reach boots can also be used, depending on the horse.

* The horse can be jumped with or without a headcollar or bridle. If a bridle is used, the reins should be tied up out of the way.

* The doors in the school should be high enough and should be closed. Mirrors should be covered up.

The different phases of the jump.

• The jumps should have wings and should form a corridor or 'lane' along the long side of the school.

• The jumps should be inviting.

• The distances between the jumps should be correct.

The trainer should have at least two assistants. It is particularly important that loose jumping is a positive experience for the horse, and it should therefore be properly conducted in an atmosphere of absolute calm. Shouting, cracking the whip unnecessarily and chasing the horse round and round are signs that the trainer does not know his job. The horse should come to see jumping as a pleasant experience, rather than jumping through fear.

After the horse has been led around for a while in walk, it should be released and allowed to loosen up and get used to the jump wings. Sending the horse down the jumping lane with the poles removed will help to give it confidence. A single jump consisting of a pole approximately 20-30cm high can then be introduced, with a placing pole in front of it. Cross-pole jumps are also good, because they teach the horse from the outset to jump the centre of the fence.

An assistant puts a lead rope on the horse and shows it the jump by walking the horse up to it. Next, he leads it towards the jump in trot, then carefully lets go as the trainer takes over and sends the horse into the jump, using his voice and whip if necessary. Another assistant, who is waiting on the short side, makes much of the horse and rewards it with some oats. A few jumps will suffice to show the horse what is required.

In large schools, leading the horse into the jump is particularly helpful in preventing it from rushing. In a smaller school it may no longer be necessary to do so once the horse is used to going over the jumps.

In the early stages, the trainer should be satisfied with sending the horse round five or six times over a single jump. The demands should be increased gradually, taking care not to overface the horse.

NOTE   The practice of making talented, keen jumpers jump high fences in the early stages of their training goes against the principles of loose jumping and can seriously undermine the horse's confidence.

Once the horse has learned to jump a single fence smoothly, the demands can be gradually increased over the next few

sessions. For example a placing pole on the ground about 3.5m before the jump will help the horse to take off at the right point. The single fence can be developed into a bounce, or a combination with one or two canter strides in between. Once the horse jumps this reliably, a staircase jump or a parallel can be built about 7m beyond it.

In jumping training, the height of the jumps should depend on the horse's ability and should be such that the horse continues to enjoy its work. The types of jump and the distances depend on the purpose of the training. Slightly longer distances and spread fences (e.g. staircase jumps) encourage the horse to stretch and 'open out' over the jump. Shorter distances and upright fences, on the other hand, make the horse shorten its strides.

4.5 Dressage Training (Basic Flatwork)

The training programme

Training a horse is not simply a matter of 'breaking it in'. It is more a programme of systematic physical education, or a 'gymnasticising' process, aimed at developing to the full the horse's natural physical and mental aptitudes and making it into an obedient riding horse with a broadly based training, and one which is a pleasure to ride.

The training programme (also known as the 'Scales of Training') sets out, in the order they are obtained, the basic qualities of the riding horse and the phases in the

The three main stages of training and the links between the different concepts.

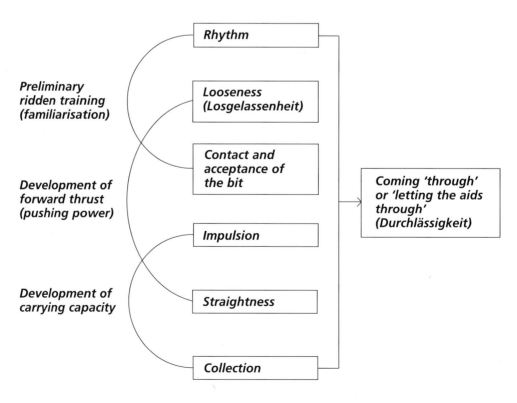

Preliminary ridden training (familiarisation)

Development of forward thrust (pushing power)

Development of carrying capacity

Rhythm

Looseness (Losgelassenheit)

Contact and acceptance of the bit

Impulsion

Straightness

Collection

Coming 'through' or 'letting the aids through' (Durchlässigkeit)

development of these qualities.

None of the six qualities can be considered in isolation – they are all interdependent. They must be developed in accordance with a systematic plan, though not singly and in a rigid order. The diagram opposite shows how the three main stages of training overlap and the

> **NOTE**   The training of every horse should meet the criteria of the recommended plan, irrespective of the horse's intended use. A horse trained accordingly will respond obediently, harmoniously and without tension to the rider's aids.

links between the different concepts. For a dressage horse, the qualities set out in this programme are essential. However, horses which are intended mainly for show jumping or cross-country work, and even leisure horses, should still receive the same systematic basic training to ensure that they are sufficiently supple and 'through' at all times (Durchlässigkeit). This ensures that they can be ridden harmoniously and also helps to keep them sound.

This training programme can be used for both:
* the systematic basic training of the young horse
* as a basis for a training session with an older horse (i.e. each individual lesson contains this training plan in a condensed form).

> **NOTE**   The attainment of these training goals depends on the horse undergoing an all-round gymnastic training ('gymnasticising'), and on the trainer being mentally attuned to the horse.

Great emphasis should be placed throughout on variety in the training. When jumping and riding across country, the rider can, and should, still be working at developing and confirming the basic qualities set out in the training plan.

A horse which is supple and 'through' (Durchlässigkeit) as a result of correct training is more obedient and agile, and is a pleasure to ride. This applies to all horses, whatever they are used for, and not just to competition horses.

> **NOTE**   The overall aim of training is a horse which is supple and 'through', i.e. 'lets the aids through' (Durchlässigkeit). The development of this quality runs parallel to that of the other qualities.

Rhythm

The term 'rhythm' refers to the regularity of the steps or strides in each gait: they should cover equal distances and also be of equal duration. For example, in working trot, the step taken by one diagonal should cover the same amount of ground as the other, and the beat should be regular.

To be able to judge the correctness of the rhythm, the trainer needs a good understanding of how the horse moves in the basic gaits (see Section 4.3).

> **NOTE**   The rhythm should be maintained through transitions and turns as well as on straight lines. No exercise or movement can be good if the rhythm falters; and the training is incorrect if it results in loss of rhythm.

Looseness (Losgelassenheit)

Looseness is a prerequisite for all further training and, along with rhythm, is an essential aim of the preliminary training phase. Even if the rhythm is maintained, the movement cannot be considered correct unless the horse is working through its back, and the muscles are free from tension.

Only if the horse is physically and mentally free from tension or constraint (in German: *Zwanglosigkeit*) can it work with looseness and can it use itself to the full.

The horse's joints should bend and straighten equally on each side of its body and with each step or stride, and the horse should convey the impression that it is putting its whole mind and body into its work.

Indications of looseness (and mental relaxation) are:
* a contented, happy expression (eyes, ear movements)
* a rhythmically swinging back
* a closed but not immobile mouth (the horse should mouth the bit gently)
* tail lifted slightly ('carried') and swinging in time with the movement
* 'snorting', which is a sign that the horse is mentally relaxed.

NOTE Looseness has been achieved when the horse will stretch its head and neck forwards and downwards in all three gaits. A horse working with looseness should swing through its back and move with rhythmic, unspoilt natural paces; it should not rush forwards, quickening its steps, i.e. 'running'. It should accept the forward-driving aids, and the rider should be able to sit the movement and not be thrown out of the saddle.

Contact

Contact is the soft, steady connection between the rider's hand and the horse's mouth. The horse should go rhythmically forward from the rider's driving aids and 'seek' a contact with the rider's hand, thus 'going onto' the contact. As they say in Germany, 'the horse seeks the contact and the rider provides it'.

A correct, steady contact allows the horse to find its balance under the rider and find a rhythm in each of the gaits. The poll should always be the highest point of the neck, except when the horse is being ridden forwards and downwards, i.e. in an extended outline.

NOTE The contact should never be achieved through a backward action of the hands; it should result from the correctly delivered forward thrust of the hind legs. The horse should go forward confidently onto the contact in response to the rider's driving aids.

Taking a contact gradually evolves into being **on the bit,** which entails flexion at the poll. This should not be considered as an aim in itself: the horse should come onto the bit as a consequence and by-product of correct schooling. When working with young horses at the basic stage of training, or when performing 'loosening' work with older horses, the trainer should avoid trying to 'get the horse onto the bit' prematurely. If this is achieved by use of the hands alone, it detracts from the looseness and the activity of the hind legs and so defeats the object of the training.

Impulsion

A horse is said to have impulsion when the energy created by the hind legs is being transmitted into the gait and into every aspect of the forward movement. A horse can be said to be working with impulsion when it pushes off energetically from the ground and swings its feet well forward.

To be able to work with impulsion in trot and canter, the horse needs first to be able to show looseness (Losgelassenheit), a springy, swinging back, and a soft, correct contact. Impulsion is only possible in the trot and canter. There can be no impulsion in the walk because there is no moment of suspension.

The impulsion is of good quality if the hocks are carried energetically forwards and upwards immediately after the feet leave the ground, rather than being carried only upwards, or being drawn backwards. The movements are absorbed by the horse's back muscles, so that the rider can sit softly and 'go with' the movement, while still feeling the powerful forward thrust of the hind legs: the horse is said to 'take the rider with it'.

> **NOTE**   Impulsion is created by training. The rider makes use of the horse's natural paces, but 'adds' to them looseness, forward thrust (originating in the hindquarters) and suppleness (Durchlässigkeit).

If the horse is pushed too hard so that it quickens its steps, the moment of suspension (suspension phase) is shortened because it puts its feet down sooner. Even if the rhythm is maintained, if the tempo is too fast the impulsion will suffer as a result.

Straightness

A horse is said to be straight when its forehand is in line with its hindquarters, that is, when its longitudinal axis is in line with the straight or curved track it is following. In Germany, the horse is then also said to be 'covering the track'.

Straightness is necessary in order for the weight to be evenly distributed over the two halves of the body. It is developed through systematically training and suppling ('gymnasticising') both sides of the body equally.

Most horses are naturally crooked. Like right- and left-handedness in humans, this crookedness has its origins in the brain and is something the horse is born with. Also, the horse's shoulders are narrower than its hindquarters which further encourages it to be crooked.

In most cases, the right hind foot is set down further to the right than the right forefoot. As a result, the right hind leg has to push forward more while the left hind leg is required to bend more. Also, the left foreleg is subjected to more wear and tear.

If more weight is transferred onto the hindquarters, so that the hind legs are required to bend more, the left hind leg will be able to bend but the right leg will try to avoid doing so by stepping sideways, outside the track of the right forefoot.

Straightness is necessary for the following reasons:

* so that the horse's weight is evenly distributed on both sides, and to avoid excessive wear and tear on the limbs on one side

* so that the horse can push equally and effectively with its hind legs (to optimise the forward thrust)

* so that the rider can keep the horse on the aids properly, and develop its suppleness (Durchlässigkeit)

* to enable the horse to have an even contact on both sides

* in order to obtain collection.

Only if the horse is straight can it be equally supple and 'through' (Durchlässigkeit) on both reins.

> **NOTE**   If the horse is straight, the hind legs will push exactly in the direction of the centre of gravity. The restraining aids will then also pass through the horse correctly, via the mouth, poll, neck and back to the hindquarters, and they will act on both hind legs equally.

Straightening the horse is a never-ending task, since every horse has some degree of natural crookedness.

Straightness is a precondition for collection since only if the horse is straight can the weight be transferred onto both hind legs equally.

Collection

The aim of all gymnastic training is to create a horse which is useful and ready and willing to perform. For the horse to meet these conditions, its weight, plus that of its rider, must be distributed as evenly as possible over all four legs. This means reducing the amount of weight on the forelegs, which naturally carry more of the load than the hind legs, and increasing by the same amount the weight on the hind legs, which were originally intended mainly for creating the forward movement.

In collection, the hind legs (the hock and stifle joints) bend more, stepping further underneath the horse in the direction of the centre of gravity, and taking a greater share of the load. This in its turn lightens the forehand, giving more freedom to the movements of the forelegs. The horse looks and feels more 'uphill'.

The steps become shorter but without losing their energy or activity. The impulsion is maintained in full in the trot and canter, and as a result the steps become more expressive and 'stately'.

> **NOTE**   The horse is built in such a way that there is more weight on its forehand than on its hindquarters. By sitting just behind the shoulders, and so placing even more weight on the forehand, the rider makes the weight distribution even more uneven. Hence training the horse to carry more of the weight on its hindquarters also makes it safer to ride (allowing it to balance and keep its footing), and helps to keep it sound. Every horse will therefore benefit from some degree of collection.

By training and developing the relevant muscles, it is possible to increase the carrying capacity of the hindquarters. On the other hand, the forelegs, which support rather than push, can only be strengthened to a very limited degree through training. It is therefore more sensible, and indeed necessary, to transfer some of the weight to the hindquarters.

The increased flexion of the hind legs results in the neck being raised. The horse is then in a position, if the carrying capacity of the hindquarters is sufficiently developed, to move in balance and **self-carriage** in all three gaits.

'Through', 'Letting the aids through' (Durchlässigkeit)

Being 'through', or 'letting the aids through', means that the horse is prepared to accept the rider's aids obediently and without tension. It should respond to the driving aids without hesitation, i.e. its hind legs should 'swing through' actively, creating forward thrust. At the same time the rein aids should pass through, i.e. be 'allowed through' from the mouth, via the poll, neck and back, to the hindquarters, without being blocked by tension at any point.

> **NOTE** The horse can be said to be 'through' or to 'let the aids through' (*durchlässig*) when it remains loose (*losgelassen*) and responds obediently, and equally on both reins, to the driving, restraining and sideways-acting aids. This quality is the hallmark of the correctly schooled horse.

A horse which can be collected at any time and in all three gaits has attained the highest level of (*Durchlässigkeit*).

Preliminary training (familiarisation)

The lessons taught in the first few weeks form the basis not only of the preliminary stage of the young horse's training, but also of the 'loosening' (*Losgelassenheit*) or warming-up process which constitutes the first phase of each training session.

The first step is to **establish a rhythm.** As a starting point, the horse should be ridden in the basic pace best suited to it, and the rider should push smoothly, evenly and in a rhythm, with a quiet, low, elastic hand. However, if the horse is ridden forward incorrectly, it will simply quicken its steps ('running') and lose rhythm. 'Riding forwards' means stimulating the hind legs to propel the body actively and powerfully forward – it does not mean increasing the pace and tempo. Regularity, in all three gaits, takes precedence over all else.

The main problems are faults in the sequence or timing of the footfalls, for example a 'pace-like' walk (tending towards two-time), or a four-time canter. In trot the commonest problems are short, irregular, tense steps, or so-called 'hovering' steps. Usually rhythm faults and loss of rhythm are caused by using too much hand and not enough leg.

Loosening exercises can be helpful, including frequent transitions and getting the horse to take the rein forward and downward. Lungeing, work over cavalletti, and possibly gymnastic jumping, or even riding across country, can all be beneficial if done correctly.

Looseness (*Losgelassenheit*) is a central theme running through the schooling. It should never be neglected, and should be constantly checked and reinforced.

Before trying to obtain looseness in the ridden work, the trainer should ensure that the horse is happy and free from mental tension. This can be achieved through regular, sensitive care and handling, and sufficient exercise. Once the horse is mentally relaxed, i.e. mentally 'loosened', external, physical 'looseness' comes relatively quickly.

Loosening exercises serve to warm up the muscles, tendons and joints, as well as to make the horse work through its back. They also stimulate the hind legs to engage and 'swing through' more. The horse should stretch towards the bit and take a confident contact.

When problems arise at a later stage in the horse's schooling, the trainer should go back to the loosening exercises again. Most training faults have more than one cause and need to be looked at as a whole. Usually, however, looseness (*Losgelassenheit*) is involved in one way or another, and the horse has not been ridden correctly. Lack of looseness can take many different forms, e.g. tightness in the back, rhythm faults, hind legs lacking activity, a tense, dry mouth and crookedness.

> **NOTE**   Rhythm (regularity and purity of the gait) and looseness (freedom from constraint) are the criteria by which every exercise should be judged.

In the preliminary training and while warming up and loosening up at other times, the horse should first be ridden on a **light contact.** The rider should not use his hands to try to force the horse to come onto the bit. It is with a light contact that the horse can most easily find its balance and begin to develop rhythm and looseness under the rider. This applies both to young and more experienced horses.

The horse should go into the reins and seek a contact with the bit in response to the rider's driving aids, and encouraged by the sensitive use of his hands.

When the horse first comes onto the contact, it will be with a relatively low position of the head and neck, i.e. with the mouth approximately level with the point of the shoulder. This is the best position for teaching the horse to stretch and relax its neck and back muscles.

Rhythm and looseness are essential for jumping and riding across country as well as in dressage. The horse needs to be able to canter in a rhythm in order to come into the fence correctly, in balance, and at a steady pace. A horse which works with looseness is able and ready to perform and to use itself. Without looseness the horse cannot 'bascule' and use its back when jumping.

A jumper which is working correctly, i.e. with looseness, will be able to help itself, and will not be put off its stride if the rider makes a mistake, or is in a difficult situation. A tense horse, on the other hand, will hesitate, jump with a stiff back, or even refuse.

Developing the forward thrust

Developing the forward thrust, or 'pushing power', involves stimulating the hind legs to work more actively and engage further underneath the horse's body towards the centre of gravity. Forward thrust is required before the carrying capacity of the hindquarters can be developed, i.e. before more of the weight can be transferred onto the hindquarters.

The horse is said to be on the **contact** when it is going forward into its bridle, irrespective of the length of its frame. The frame will become shorter as the forward thrust develops, and the hind legs engage further under the body. The horse will then be prepared and able to raise and arch its neck more and flex at the poll, bringing its nose close to the vertical. If the trainer ignores this principle, and attempts to force the horse into a shorter outline, he will simply block the activity of the horse's back and hind legs. Hence, when judging whether or not the horse is correctly on the contact or 'on the bit', it is not enough to look only at the head and neck. You need to look at the whole horse, its position and carriage and in particular the way it moves.

Unfortunately, mistakes are frequently made when teaching the horse to come onto the contact. These result in many different faults, the commonest of which are as follows:

Nose behind the vertical – Going with the nose behind the vertical is caused by using the hands too strongly. This fault may result either from a momentary mistake in applying the aids or it may be a symptom of long term incorrect schooling. The only way to correct it is by pushing the horse forward and at the same time yielding with the hands.

Behind the contact, dropping the contact – With this problem, not only is the horse's nose behind the vertical but also the horse evades the action of the bit by backing off from the contact: it refuses to go into its bridle. Often, at the same time, the head is flexed from a vertebra further down the neck rather than at the poll (see 'false bend').

The first step is to re-establish the contact. The horse must learn to have confidence in the rider's hand. The trainer will usually need to start by riding on a long rein. Skilful lungeing can also be beneficial, and riding actively forwards, especially out of doors, sometimes helps to get the horse to stretch forward onto the contact.

To correct this fault, the rider needs to be especially sensitive in his coordination of the driving and restraining aids. The correct hand position is important, as is the straight line through the forearm, hand and rein. It is only possible to 'push the nose forward' if the hands are soft and elastic, and carried low. On no account

should the rider try to raise the head by carrying his hands high.

False bend – This occurs as a result of the rider attempting to establish the contact by acting in a backward direction with his hands. The highest point of the neck is no longer the poll but a point further back, usually between the third and fourth vertebrae.

This is a serious fault which can only be corrected by lengthy, systematic reschooling. While riding the horse energetically forward, the trainer needs to be able to prevent rhythm faults or hurrying by elastic use of his hands, and at the same time to 'give' sufficiently with his hands to allow the neck to adopt the correct outline.

'Taking the rein forward and downward' is a good exercise for horses with this fault. The horse needs to learn all over again how to stretch the topline of its neck and to go forwards onto the contact.

Leaning on the bit – The horse seeks support from the rider's hands, using them as a 'fifth foot', because it is not working sufficiently from behind. The rider needs to stimulate the hind legs to greater activity by increasing his driving aids.

Judiciously 'asking' and yielding

Correct

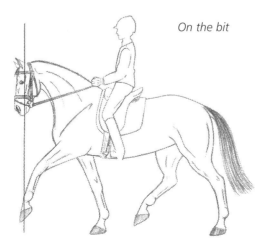

On the bit

Incorrect

Behind the vertical

Behind the contact

False bend – flexion is from a point behind the poll

Against the hand, above the bit.

Leaning on the bit

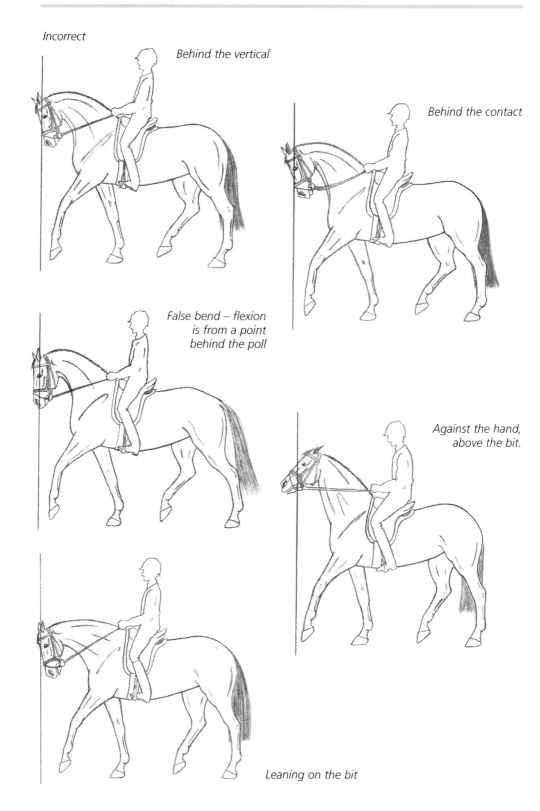

alternately with the hands, and riding frequent transitions with a sensitive hand can be effective against this fault. On no account should the rider 'offer' his hands as a support.

Against the hand, above the bit – In this fault the horse's nose is well in front of the vertical. The horse will not flex at the poll and uses the muscles on the underside of the neck to resist the hand, while at the same time stiffening and hollowing its back. If this is a long-standing fault, and the wrong muscles have been allowed to develop, lungeing with side-reins can be very beneficial. The side-reins should be shortish at first, and then gradually lengthened. This work teaches the horse to stretch and work in a longer outline, without the additional problem of the rider's weight on its back. The correct musculature will then gradually develop.

When correcting this fault under saddle, the trainer should take particular trouble over the warming-up phase of the lesson, and should spend extra time on 'loosening' exercises. If the horse is loose (Losgelassenheit) and swings through its back it will be able to establish a good contact. Riding in an extended outline, i.e. frequently getting the horse to stretch forward and down, will enable the correct musculature to develop. Use of the opening rein (sideways-acting rein) may help to 'show the horse the way to the ground' (teach it to stretch downwards). The best way to achieve this is to ride on gentle curves and large circles, changing the rein frequently.

With some horses, because of the conformation and the shape of the neck, when the horse is in an extended outline and yielding at the poll as required, the nose is slightly behind the vertical. In this case the trainer must ensure that the activity of the hind legs is maintained. On no account should he weaken or shorten the horse's neck, i.e. 'pull the horse together'. This would simply create tension and, since the neck is the horse's 'balancing pole', seriously disturb the horse's balance. It is therefore impossible to obtain looseness by this method.

Impulsion can be developed and improved by riding transitions from one gait to another and within a gait. Special emphasis should be placed on maintaining the rhythm through the transitions, and on sensitive use of the rein aids during the downward transitions so as not to restrict the forward movement of the hind legs and prevent them from 'swinging through'.

Impulsion should not be confused with the term 'action', which simply refers to the horse's inherent ability to take expressive, ground-covering trot steps, for example. These steps may be accompanied by tension and a stiff back, and the horse may go with its head 'in the air'.

If the horse is working with impulsion, the moment of suspension will be more pronounced. However, it should not exaggerated, since this would denote incorrect **hovering steps,** which are associated with tension.

It is not only in dressage that contact and impulsion are essential. In jumping and cross-country work they enable the rider to remain constantly and harmoniously in control of the horse, the pace and the direction. As a result of impulsion, the activity of the hindquarters is increased so that the hind feet push off more energetically from the ground and the horse is able to take more efficient, ground-covering strides.

If the horse is working with impulsion it will respond correctly to the driving aids, that is, it will not hurry or fall onto the forehand but will 'let the impulsion through' from behind. The development and improvement of the impulsion is of fundamental importance, and features equally in the development of the forward thrust and of the carrying power of the hindquarters. It is also a prerequisite for straightening the horse and for collection.

The development of forward thrust is of great importance in jumping and cross-country riding, as well as in dressage. A steady, soft contact is necessary for accuracy and control, particularly when riding turns and related distances. In response to the rider's driving aids, the horse's hind legs should spring further under its body, towards the centre of gravity, so that it takes a confident contact with the rider's hand. Only then will it be able to perform a ground-covering canter. Owing to the increase in thrust, the horse's jumping power will also be greater.

Developing the carrying capacity of the hindquarters

Training aimed specifically at developing straightness and collection is not feasible

until the forward thrust is fairly well established. The rhythm in all three paces also needs to be established, along with the 'looseness' and the contact.

The development of impulsion and straightness are essential to prepare the horse for collection and to make it more supple and 'through' *(Durchlässigkeit)*. The horse must first be ridden forwards, as is clearly expressed in the quotation from Gustav Steinbrecht, a 19th-century classical horseman:

'Ride your horse forwards and position it straight.'

Impulsion is the main criterion. Aids which act in a backward direction are always incorrect. The horse is said to be straight, or straight to the track when, while working on a single track, be it straight or curved, its longitudinal axis is aligned with the track.

Preliminary work on straightness begins as soon as the young horse learns to respond to the rider's aids. However, exercises aimed specifically at developing straightness cannot begin until the forward

The horse is not yet straight. The hind feet are not treading in the prints of the forefeet.

The horse is straight. The forehand is aligned with the quarters.

thrust and impulsion have been developed, because they need to be performed with the horse going positively forwards. If the horse is crooked to the right, that is, its right hind foot follows a track outside that of the right forefoot, this means that the right hind leg is escaping sideways in order to avoid having to bend. This causes more weight to be placed on the left shoulder, and the horse tends to lean on the left rein.

On the left side, the neck muscles are stiff, tense and unyielding. This is known as the 'stiff side'. The 'difficult side', however, is the hollow right side. The right hind leg escapes sideways, and the horse goes against the rider's right leg and refuses to go into the right rein. Schooling should be aimed at getting the right hind leg to step forwards underneath the body. The horse will then also stretch forward and take a contact on the right rein. When this happens, the stiffness on the left side will disappear of its own accord.

Exercises used for improving straightness are curved tracks and circles, leg-yielding, and later, lateral work, especially shoulder-in. These are all exercises which increase the horse's obedience to the leg. Likewise, counter-canter is also beneficial.

Straightness should always be achieved by aligning the forehand with the hindquarters, and not the quarters with the forehand. For example, if the right hind foot is escaping to the side, the rider should use his right leg to prevent the horse stepping any further to the side, and his left leg, closer to the girth, to make the left hind foot step further forward. The left hand should be held low, with the left rein regulating, or 'guarding', the outside shoulder, while the right hand guides the forehand to the right until the right fore foot is in front of the right hind foot.

Collection is only achieved through correctly structured training, patience and dedication.

Provided the horse is working with impulsion, riding transitions on straight and curved tracks will improve the straightness and collection. The forward thrust increases as a result of the rider pushing. However, instead of 'giving' with his hand and allowing the energy to flow forwards, as in lengthening the strides, the rider uses what is more a non-yielding or 'asking' rein aid, and 'catches up' the energy, which is then passed back through a supple back to the hindquarters. As a result, the weight-carrying capacity of the quarters is increased.

'Catching up' the energy requires skilful, sensitive use of the hands so as not to restrict the forward swing of the horse's hind legs. Any exercise which teaches the horse to carry more weight on its hindquarters is a **collecting** exercise, i.e. an exercise which increases the collection. Correctly performed half-halts and transitions to halt are prime examples.

The difference between a 'collecting' exercise and a 'collected' exercises lies in the manner in which it is performed. During basic training, the rein-back, for example, is ridden at first as a 'collecting' exercise. The head and neck can be lower so as to allow the horse to use its back more. In advanced training, the head and neck should be carried higher and the horse should be in self-carriage. This is a **collected** exercise.

As a basic rule, in between periods of collecting or straightening work, the rider should ride actively forwards in order to preserve the **purity of the gait.** The quality of the collection training can be judged by sending the horse forward into medium trot after a period of collected trot, and assessing the correctness and rhythm of the gait. If the horse leans on

The quality of the medium trot reflects the quality of the horse's overall training.

the bit or loses rhythm, or resists the leg (thereby stiffening in its back and poll), this means that the collection training has been incorrectly performed or the trainer has asked for too much. If, on the other hand, the horse takes rhythmical, expressive strides, this is a sign that the collection training was being carried out correctly so that the horse is ready and able to carry the rider forward with looseness, rhythm and impulsion into the medium trot, while maintaining a light contact and lengthening its outline in keeping with the longer, more ground-covering strides. In the transition back to collected trot, if the horse has been correctly schooled, the impulsion from the medium trot will 'carry through' into the collected trot, resulting in higher, more cadenced steps.

Cadence means that the moment of suspension is more clearly defined. However, the hind legs must 'swing through' and engage well underneath the horse, otherwise incorrect hovering steps will occur, which are a sign of tension and stiffness in the back.

The duration of the collected work or collection training depends on how fit the horse is. If overdone, it simply leads to tension and resistance.

The head carriage is directly related to the collection. The horse should move with its head and neck raised in accordance with the degree of collection, or in dressage parlance, with its head and neck **relatively raised.**

Hence a horse which is on the bit but carrying less weight on its quarters will carry its head and neck lower, and its neck will be longer. As the weight on the quarters increases, that is, as the collection increases, the forehand becomes lighter. The hindquarters are lowered as a result of the increased flexion, making the horse look higher in front and so slightly 'uphill'. With correct training, this carriage develops naturally.

Raising the head mainly by use of the hands is incorrect. The head carriage is no longer related to the degree of engagement. In dressage parlance, the head and neck are said to be raised **absolutely,** as opposed to relatively.

In collection, there is increased flexion of the haunches. The hind legs step further forward under the body (in the direction of the centre of gravity), and the horse moves in self-carriage with its head and neck raised in proportion to the degree of collection ('relatively raised').

Instead of the horse being in self-carriage, the rider is supporting the head and neck, and the activity of the hindquarters is restricted because the horse is not working correctly through its back.

If the carrying capacity of the hindquarters is sufficiently developed, the horse will be able to balance itself and move in self-carriage in any gait, notwithstanding the rider's weight. The rider can test this balance by 'giving and retaking the reins' for a few strides. The horse should remain in self-carriage.

'Letting the aids through' *(Durchlässigkeit)* is the result of correct, gymnastic schooling ('gymnasticising'). If the horse possesses *Durchlässigkeit,* this is conclusive evidence that the training has been correct.

'Letting the aids through' is closely related to, and interconnected with, the other aims of training:

* It allows the rhythm to be maintained reliably in all three gaits, and also in the transitions.

* Only if the horse moves with 'looseness' *(Losgelassenheit)* can the energy from the hindquarters pass forward through the horse's body. Also, without 'looseness' it is impossible for the restraining aids to act, via the mouth, poll, neck and back, on the hindquarters.

* Any problems in the contact, that is, unsteadiness or stiffness in the connection between the rider's hand and the horse's mouth, will interfere with the horse's ability to 'let the aids through'.

* A horse which works with impulsion, which is supple through its back, and so 'swings through' with its hind legs, will be in a better position to let both the driving and the restraining aids through.

* Not until the horse becomes straighter can it perform half-halts equally on both reins, and at the same time go more positively onto the contact in response to the rider's driving aids, without its hind legs escaping to the side.

* This, in its turn, is absolutely essential for collection and consequently for the correct raising of the head and neck.

* If the horse responds correctly to the exercises in collection by stepping forward more, and with both hind legs equally, in the direction of the centre of gravity, and by taking more weight on its hindquarters as required, this is an indication that it has achieved a high degree of *Durchlässigkeit*.

Straightness, collection and the ability to 'let the aids through' are also necessary for advanced or more demanding jumping and cross-country work and training. They make it possible to ride an accurate course and to control the pace in any situation, that is, to lengthen and shorten the stride as required. They also ensure, in jumping and cross-country horses as well as dressage horses, that the weight is evenly distributed over the limbs.

Dressage schooling is necessary for every riding horse whether it is intended for use in dressage, jumping, cross-country or leisure riding.

The horse should receive an all-round education which should contain plenty of variety. However, dressage training is always the starting point although it should be supplemented, for example, by work over cavalletti or by being ridden outdoors.

As soon as the horse has learned through its initial training to respond to the aids, special emphasis should be placed on the development of rhythm and looseness. The horse needs to learn to work in balance in the three basic gaits, at a steady pace and on a light contact

Training in walk

At the beginning of its training, the young horse needs to learn to walk calmly and get used to the rider's forward-driving aids. As a general rule, only the long rein walk, on a light contact, should be used for the first few months, otherwise the walk can all too easily become irregular.

The rider should allow the natural nodding movement of the horse's head and neck, and should 'give' in his elbow and shoulder joints sufficiently not to restrict the horse's natural length of stride.

Asking the horse to come onto the contact too early in walk, or 'placing' the horse's head with the hands, can seriously affect the regularity and the length of stride, as well as leading to tension. These fault can be very difficult to correct.

Incorrect use of the legs, as well as the hands, spoils the walk. Constantly squeezing or tapping or keeping the legs clamped against the horse's sides disturbs the rhythm and also makes the horse unresponsive, or 'dead to the legs'. On a lazy horse, the whip or spurs should be used briefly to reinforce the action of the leg and make the horse more responsive to the aids.

Holding the lower legs so that they are not in contact with the horse will make it hesitant or over-reactive. A tense, nervous horse will calm down more quickly if the legs are held quietly in contact with its sides.

The horse should be ridden in a walk on a long rein for the first 10-15 minutes of each training session, before starting the trot and canter work. This helps to make it mentally relaxed, and ensures that the joints, tendons and muscles are warmed up gradually.

The horse should frequently be given the opportunity to walk on a loose rein in between periods of trot and canter. This makes it easier for a young horse to cope with the unfamiliar work, and in the case of older horses, it provides an opportunity to relax both mentally and physically in between different elements of the training session.

Training in trot

Only rising trot should be used in the first few weeks of a young horse's training, until it can move with looseness (*Losgelassenheit*) and has found its balance to some extent in this gait. The horse should be ridden forwards, but without hurrying, on straight lines and large diameter curved tracks. This teaches it to accept the rider's driving aids.

Being ridden forwards onto a soft contact and through a swinging back serves to develop the forward thrust of the quarters. Trot is the gait in which it is easiest for the young horse to learn to take a contact.

Once the rhythm and the contact are established, the trainer can try briefly increasing the strides and then decreasing them again by means of sensitively applied half-halts. It is important not to ask for too much at this stage: a few lengthened strides are enough.

Rising trot is used to ease the weight on the back muscles and to make it easier for them to contract and extend. Sitting trot should be introduced gradually, and for short periods to start with. Changing frequently from rising to sitting trot and back again is a particularly effective way of getting the horse used to the sitting trot, and also prevents the muscles from becoming tired or tense.

Training in canter

Canter work can be introduced after a few lessons, when the horse can be ridden on turns and large circles in trot. In the early stages, if the horse offers to canter of its own accord, the trainer should take advantage of this opportunity and allow it to do so.

Most horses find it easier to canter with the left leg leading than with the right. For this reason, the easiest way to obtain a strike-off into canter is to ride the horse on a left-hand circle in trot, and to ask for the strike-off into canter on arriving at the wall after passing through the centre of the school. The rider should encourage the horse to canter by riding it forwards and pushing more with his inside leg. A touch with the whip can also be helpful to start with, to reinforce these aids. If the horse speeds up in trot instead of striking off into canter, it should first be brought back to a steady trot before being asked again to canter.

After a few successful strike-offs into left canter, the trainer should start working on the canter on the right leg. On no account should the horse be punished if it strikes off on the wrong leg since this would simply lead to tension rather than serving to re-balance the horse in preparation for the correct strike-off. It may help to flex the horse to the outside slightly just before the strike-off. This changes the weight distribution in such a way that the horse is encouraged to strike off on the inside leg.

The horse should be cantered only for short periods to start with, and the rider should not put too much weight in the saddle. Changing to the light seat after the strike-off will help the horse to stay in balance with the rider.

Once the canter is relatively well established, the trainer can practise increasing and decreasing the strides. This will teach the horse to engage more with its inside hind leg, and the upward and downward transitions within the canter will result in greater impulsion and roundness. The rider must avoid 'bombarding' the horse with the driving aids in an attempt to make it lengthen its strides. The aim of increasing the driving aids is to stimulate the horse gradually to 'swing through' more with its hind legs.

Frequent transitions should be performed from trot to canter and back again. These transitions are particularly good for developing looseness and suppleness, and for getting the horse to 'let the aids through' (Durchlässigkeit).

Upward and downward **transitions,** both from one gait to another and within a gait, teach the horse to use its hind legs more actively in response to the rider's driving aids and to swing through its back.

Asking the horse for a sudden transition will make it difficult for it to keep its balance. If, to start with, the horse is given a few moments to understand and respond to the rider's aids, and is then praised, it will learn more quickly than if force is used. Harsh driving and restraining aids will simply upset the horse and cause tension. The same principles apply when riding transitions to halt.

When riding **curved tracks,** the rider should start with large circles and gentle curves such as shallow loops in from the track on the long side, and three- or four-loop serpentines through the whole school. Circles should be no less than 10m in diameter. Increasing and decreasing the circle by spiralling inwards and outwards is particularly good for improving the horse's bend and suppleness. The rider needs to ensure that the horse is accepting the outside rein and working correctly into it during this exercise.

Work on two tracks, for example the different forms of leg-yielding, can be introduced as the training progresses. The

turn on the forehand is also good for teaching the horse to obey the sideways-pushing aids.

New exercises should always be ridden for short periods at first, and followed by riding actively forwards in order to re-establish the impulsion and looseness. The trainer should be satisfied if the horse obeys only partially to start with. Improving the horse's suppleness and obedience to the aids is of greater value than getting the horse to perform the exercise accurately but mechanically.

During the basic training, the aim of the riding-in or 'loosening' phase of the lesson is to get the horse to meet basic, essential training criteria (e.g. looseness), which will then form a basis for, and underlie, the main or 'working' phase of the lesson, during which the new material is gradually and progressively introduced. Hence during the main part of the lesson the horse should still be allowed to 'take the rein forward and downward' at regular intervals, as a test of the rhythm, looseness, contact and impulsion. The final, 'relaxation and recovery' phase of the lesson should always be long enough to allow the horse to return to its stable relaxed and in a positive frame of mind.

Once the necessary degree of suppleness has been achieved through basic dressage schooling, the trainer can start work on teaching the horse **Straightness to the track on curved tracks** (i.e. aligning the horse correctly with the curved track), as well as on **Collection**. Frequently alternating between easier and more difficult work, and between collected and more extended forms of the gait, will help to keep the horse calm and happy, and to maintain the impulsion. It is a mistake to maintain collection for long periods with young horses. Only by continually riding the horse forward out of the collection can the trainer ensure that it will always be prepared to step forwards, with both hind feet equally, in the direction of its centre of gravity, and carry itself and its rider forward.

The periods of collected work may gradually be increased as the horse becomes fitter and the musculature more developed. Doing too much leads to tension and possibly resistance, and never gives the desired result.

The **exercises** should be progressive. Often, through ignorance, horses are asked to do things they are not ready for. Since they are not supple enough and have not received sufficient gymnastic training, they can then only perform these exercises in a tense, constrained fashion. The first priority is to ensure that the horse understands the basic aids which will be used in the new exercise. For example, the counter-canter should not be attempted until the horse will remain consistently on the aids in canter and can perform a few strides of collection. If the horse is not ready for the exercise, it will become upset and, for example, rush forward, become disunited, or even come off the aids altogether. The trainer must use his 'feel' and his knowledge to decide when the horse is in a position to understand the new demands and when it is ready to perform the new exercise 'of its own accord', as it were.

> **NOTE**   Throughout training, the exercises are not an end in themselves but merely a gauge of the success of the training so far and of the suppleness *(Durchlässigkeit)* of the horse.

If the horse responds obediently and without stiffening to the forward-driving, restraining, sideways-pushing and regulating aids, it will have no problem coping with the basic dressage exercises. These exercises are not an end in themselves, but should fall into the rider's lap 'like a ripe fruit', if the training is correct and as the suppleness increases. If misunderstandings arise between horse and rider during the training, it is almost always necessary to lower the demands and to go back and check the basic training. Often one step on the ladder has been neglected so that something is missing from the overall picture of the 'correctly trained horse'. The horse will not then be in a position to do what is asked of it.

It usually takes about two years to complete the horse's basic training on the flat. Depending on the horse, however, this phase may sometimes last longer.

> **NOTE**   Only if the trainer constantly bears in mind the concepts which form the basis of the training will he be able to produce a horse which is supple and 'lets the aids through'.

4.6 Jumping Training

Jumping is a integral part of the young horse's gymnastic training. Depending on the horse's suitability, it may then go on to specialise in this area, but it should first, in any case, receive a sound basic education.

Familiarising the horse with different surroundings, jumps and types of terrain should be tied in with its dressage training. Not only will this increase the horse's usefulness and controllability in any situation, but the gymnastic jumping exercises and the cross-country work will contribute greatly to its agility, suppleness and obedience.

NOTE An all-round basic training, carried out knowledgeably and with sensitivity, is the best way to ensure the horse's soundness and well-being.

The horse should be ridden throughout its jumping training by an experienced, tactful rider. Rider-induced mistakes can lead to loss of confidence or even serious resistance.

A few weeks after being backed, and when the horse has received some preliminary training on the flat, work over **cavalletti** can be introduced. The trainer should start by riding the horse in walk and trot over single cavalletti in the low position. However little the horse has been asked to do, the rider should still reward it and make much of it since this is the best way to build its confidence. Once the horse will walk and trot calmly, and in a long outline, over single cavalletti, more can be gradually added to form a row.

It is better to include some jumping in as many of the training sessions as possible than to dedicate one session per week to intensive jumping training.

The rows of cavalletti can be set out either in a straight line or on a circle. The latter is recommended when several horses with different lengths of stride are working together since it allows the distances to be varied to suit the stride. During basic training only normal distances should be used, but with more experienced horses increasing and decreasing the distances can help to increase the length of the strides and to make the horse bend its joints more.

Single cavalletti in the high position should be jumped out of canter. This work, along with the early lessons in loose jumping, forms the basis for the jumping training.

Work over cavalletti is an excellent gymnastic exercise both for young horses and for older, more experienced jumping horses. It can be performed, in moderation, on an almost daily basis without overtaxing the horse. The rider should use his experience to guide him in selecting the layouts, distances, heights and combinations of cavalletti which will

Trotting over cavalletti.

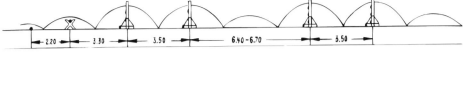

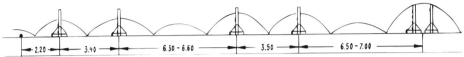

Two examples of grids. (Further examples can be found in Section 3.3.)

be of most benefit to his horse. He should be able to feel when the horse is becoming more supple and elastic and when it is time to bring the lesson to a close. Cavalletti should never be placed on top of one another since jumps constructed in this way can cause accidents.

After four to six months, when the horse has received basic training on the flat and also been introduced to cavalletti, hacking and basic loose jumping, the trainer can begin the actual jumping training.

The aim of gymnastic **jumping training** is to develop the motor skills necessary for jumping, without putting unnecessary physical strain on the horse. The horse should first be jumped over small single fences with or without a trotting pole in front. Cross-pole fences are good because they teach the horse from the outset to jump in the centre. During the basic training, it is a good idea to use wings, both on single fences and in grids. They help to prevent the horse from running out and make it jump more purposefully.

An experienced rider will ensure from the outset that after the jump, as well as before it, the horse maintains a steady pace and an even rhythm, and follows the intended track. Attention to these points

will result in a horse which is more supple and 'through' *(Durchlässigkeit)* and will make the rest of the jumping training easier.

When the horse will jump single fences calmly and in a rhythm, it can be introduced to rows of jumps, or **grids.** These should be made up of low jumps, and the distances between the jumps should be suited to the horse. To begin with, two or three jumps and a placing pole are enough, to be jumped out of trot.

When riding over grids the rider should accompany the horse's movement with an elastic seat and maintain as steady a position as possible, with his weight off the horse's back. If the rider is constantly changing his position, it is more difficult for the horse to keep its balance.

It is especially important at this stage that the horse gains confidence and enjoys its work, and that it is not asked to do too much. Simply jumping the same fences over and over again is unproductive. Confidence in its rider and variety in its work will keep the horse happy and make it willing to give of its best.

The **layout of the grid** and the type of jumps used depends on what the trainer is trying to achieve:

* To make the horse **use its back** the

jumps should be inviting and confidence-inspiring. The spacings should match the horse's stride exactly, and on no account be too wide. A relatively short, steep trajectory over the jump will encourage the horse to arch and stretch its back from the withers, i.e. to bascule.

* Grids, containing jumps of various different types, help to develop the horse's **technique, suppleness and agility.** Upright fences and slightly shorter distances will improve the horse's foreleg technique, whereas easy spread fences, jumped at a steady pace, can be useful for improving the hind leg technique. Bounce fences can be used in the same way as grids.

* To improve the horse's **attentiveness and speed of reaction** the jumps should be made as varied as possible. Making the jumps out of different materials and training occasionally in different places over different jumps can prevent boredom and carelessness. If the horse refuses to listen or take an interest, this may be because it has been asked to do too much.

* To teach the horse to size up or assess the fence and **see its stride,** the take-off aids (e.g. placing poles and some of the intermediate fences) should be gradually removed. The groundline or filler on the remaining fences can then be moved forward slightly to start with, to make it easier for the horse. Frequently changing the distances between the fences and varying the take-off aids can further improve the horse's ability to see its stride.

* Jumping small fences at a steady pace is particularly good for developing **power** (jumping capacity) and **spring**. Jumping from trot over a fence with a placing pole should help the horse to push off energetically and confidently, without hurrying. The horse's jumping capacity is developed by getting it to push off powerfully from a steady trot or canter, not by going faster. Bounce fences can also be useful in this respect.

* To increase the horse's **confidence** in its jumping ability and to encourage it to 'open up' over the fence, the distances between the jumps should at first be on the short side rather than too long. Very gradually increasing the distances and making low spread fences wider will, if combined with systematic schooling, enable the horse to develop the necessary confidence. Jumps with an 'inviting' profile will make the job easier. When the distances between the fences are related, the distance allowed for each stride should be such that the rider can use his driving aids to accompany and support the horse's movement. Only if the horse is working at a steady pace and in a rhythm, and is in front of the rider's leg (i.e. in front of his driving aids) will it be able to jump with confidence.

New or unfamiliar fences and different distances often give rise to problems. The horse should be introduced to a wide range of different jumps as early as possible in its jumping training, though at this stage the jumps should be kept low. It should be familiarised gradually with new fences, especially solid ones such as post and rails, gates and walls. Using another horse to give it a lead can be helpful in the beginning. A young horse should never be forced to jump by punishing it since this will destroy rather than build its confidence.

NOTE It is important that the trainer should avoid provoking resistance during the horse's jumping training. Only through positive experiences will the horse learn to jump with confidence and enjoy its work.

As the horse becomes more proficient at jumping grids, it can be introduced to single fences with a placing pole in front. These should be jumped from trot at first, and then out of a steady canter. **Related distances,** involving curved as well as straight tracks, are good for improving the horse's suppleness and obedience, and for making it more 'through' (*Durchlässigkeit*). At this stage in the training it is particularly important that the rider is sufficiently experienced to be able to 'see a stride', so that he can help the horse if necessary by adjusting the length of stride. A young horse which has repeatedly been presented wrongly at a fence will lose confidence and become indecisive.

At a later stage in the training, **banks and ditches** can be introduced. Here again, careful preparation is necessary, and the horse should perhaps be given a lead by another, more experienced jumper.

The obstacles should be small to start with, to give the horse a chance to get used to them. The demands can then gradually be increased, and small obstacles can be added in front of and after the bank.

To prevent the horse from refusing, steps, banks and drop fences should be approached purposefully and with plenty of impulsion, though not at a faster pace. The horse should be well 'on the aids', because there is a tendency to hesitate with this sort of jump. Jumping ditches is learned through systematic, structured training, just like jumping any other obstacle. It should present no particular problems, since a jump over a ditch is essentially no more than an extra-long canter stride.

However, if the ditch has water in it, the colour and the reflection of the water will be unfamiliar to a young horse. If particular care is not taken at this stage, this sort of obstacle can become a permanent source of fear and resistance.

Bank and rails

Coffin-type fence with rails as central element.

The ditch should be as inviting as possible, and there should be wings at the ends of the section to be jumped. To begin with, a pole should be placed about 50cm above the ditch to ensure that the horse jumps high enough, and also to make it concentrate more on the pole than on the water underneath it.

A tarpaulin can be used as a substitute for the water, and has the advantage that, to start with, it can be rolled up as small as necessary. It can then be gradually unrolled and finally the water can be added.

When the horse will happily jump water-filled ditches with a pole over them, the next stage, training it to jump **coffins,** should present no problems. To start with, only the ditch element should be jumped, then the ditch and the final element, and finally all three elements.

Transitions, riding over cavalletti, turns, and halts followed by rein-back between fences, are all very useful for increasing the horse's suppleness and manoeuvrability, or 'ridability', and are required in the German 'style jumping' tests.

Next, the horse can be asked to jump slightly higher single fences. As a result of this training, and of the gymnastic jumping, it will learn relatively quickly the correct technique for jumping a **course of jumps.**

When jumping a course, the main requirements are:
* to maintain a rhythm
* to maintain a steady pace, i.e. the basic canter used for jumping
* the horse should be fit enough to jump a number of fences in rapid succession while maintaining an even pace
* the horse should be able to jump fences in the widest possible range of shapes and colours, and to do so confidently, smoothly and, on the whole, cleanly
* the horse should be able to perform changes of direction and gait, and changes of leg at canter, with suppleness *(Durchlässigkeit)* and without resistance.

When jumping a course, the rider should endeavour to canter the horse on the correct leg. When **changing direction,** with a young horse the change of leg can be through trot. However, some horses will perform a flying change spontaneously at this point in response to the change in the balance.

To get the horse used to jumping courses, small sections of the course should be ridden before the whole course is attempted. The jumps should be kept low. The main emphasis should be on maintaining an even pace throughout. Sensitive and subtle use of the aids is required to maintain the required pace, i.e. the basic canter used for jumping, which varies slightly from one horse to another. Training the horse to jump from a faster pace should be a very gradual process. A young horse should not be jumped in competitions until it can jump courses consistently in a training environment.

4.7 Cross-Country Training

Every horse should become accustomed early on in its training to being ridden outdoors. Whether it is to be used for leisure riding or for competitions, being ridden out quietly on a regular basis will keep the horse interested and relaxed. At the same time it will help to improve its balance, coordination and agility.

Regular hacking, in a group or with an experienced lead horse, is sufficient for the first few months. The rider should adopt a fairly light seat. When the horse is used to this, it can be asked to perform various exercises away from the group.

Hacking and riding out help to keep the horse **mentally well-adjusted.** Hence, if the right facilities are available, riding out can provide an excellent opportunity for a change of scene before or after a training session in the school. Walking on a long rein is particularly important. Often, the rider makes the mistake of keeping the horse on a tight rein, especially if it is

nervous. This makes the horse even more tense and nervous rather than helping to make it loose and relaxed (*Losgelassenheit*).

As part of its cross-country training, the horse can start to be ridden over **undulating terrain** when the opportunity arises. This work should be carried out in walk and trot, and later in canter. However, very steep slopes should be avoided with a young horse, since it will not be able to keep its balance at this stage.

The horse needs to learn to take undulating terrain and gentle slopes in its stride, without losing rhythm. Quiet, steady riding helps to develop the muscles of the back and hindquarters and plays a part in the overall gymnastic training, as well as making the horse use and bend its hip and stifle joints more. Riding up and down **steep slopes** and later **banks** should also be included in the training. Training should be progressive, structured and systematic, and the demands should be increased gradually. This work is tiring for the horse and should not be overdone. It is important that the horse is ridden straight (rather than obliquely) up and down steep slopes so that the hind legs carry an equal share of the weight and also to prevent the horse from slipping.

Dressage exercises can also be performed out on a ride if the going is suitable. Increasing and decreasing the stride, turns and circular tracks, leg-yielding and 'taking the rein down' will make the horse listen and help it to become more supple and 'through' (*Durchlässigkeit*).

Early training over **cross-country fences** can run parallel to the horse's training over cavalletti, grids and low single fences in the school. The only precondition is that the horse is in balance and well 'on the aids'.

The first cross-country obstacles should be chosen with care: they should be low and inviting, and the take-off and landing zones should be level and in good condition. Showing the horse the jump beforehand with will help to reassure it in the early stages. As in the rest of the jumping training, the fences should be jumped out of trot to start with. As the horse becomes more proficient, they can be jumped from a steady canter.

> **NOTE** With problem horses the trainer must always take conformation defects and weaknesses into account. Optimum results will only be achieved if the training is then adapted accordingly.

Logs and hedges with a natural barrier at the sides are particularly suitable for early cross-country training. For the first few weeks, it is enough to jump the horse over a few selected natural obstacles in order to build its confidence.

Riding a young horse hard at the fence in order to try to force it over will simply destroy its confidence. In cross-country riding mutual confidence is essential for a good relationship between horse and rider,

and ensures that risks are minimised.

Eventually, the horse needs to be able to jump **unfamiliar obstacles.** To be able to do so, it needs to satisfy the following requirements:

* it must have received basic training on the flat
* it must have received basic jumping training
* it must be accustomed to being ridden over different types of terrain
* it must be used to jumping low, familiar obstacles
* it must be basically fit
* it must have confidence in its rider

Portable cross-country fences can be used to prepare the horse for jumping unfamiliar fences. They should be made as inviting as possible and located in familiar surroundings.

Once the horse will jump the portable fence with confidence, the fence can be moved into unfamiliar surroundings. The rider should first walk the horse up to the jump, which will now look quite different to it, and allow it to inspect it. It should not be allowed to escape sideways or step back. When it will look at the fence calmly, it can be asked to jump it, at first from trot

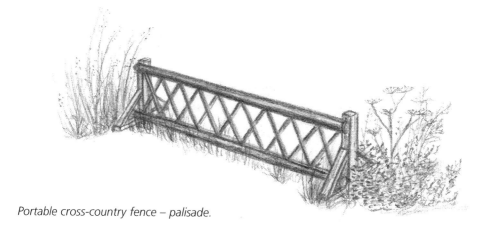

Portable cross-country fence – palisade.

Riding through water – sending an experienced horse ahead helps to give the horse confidence.

and then later from canter. When the young horse has gained its confidence in this way in a variety of different situations, it will be prepared to jump unfamiliar obstacles without first going up to them to have a look.

Riding through **shallow water** should form part of every horse's basic training, and should be practised with an experienced horse in the lead. The more gradual the slope into the water, and the shallower the water, the more readily the horse will follow the lead horse through it. If the horse is then given plenty of praise, going through water will soon present no problems. The rider should always use places he knows and which will provide a firm footing for the horse. Suddenly sinking into soft ground will cause the horse to panic, and destroy its confidence in water.

The horse can next be trotted and cantered through the water in suitable places. When it is used to this, it can be taught to jump out of the water over an

obstacle. Placing a log on the bank will teach the horse to jump out with the necessary impulsion. When jumping into the water, the trainer needs to bear in mind that the water has a braking effect on the forward momentum so that, as a basic rule, he should ride a steady, unhurried approach to prevent the horse falling. The trainer should not ask too much of a young horse to start with, so as to build its confidence.

Ditches also require systematic training. The horse should first be trained over small, dry ditches, and **given a lead** by another, more experienced horse. As with any new obstacles, the horse should first be ridden up to the ditch in walk and allowed to look at it. If the horse is nervous to start with, the trainer should use patience and a reasoned approach rather than force. Experience shows that, with ditches of all things, it pays to go very slowly. This will build the horse's confidence, whereas asking for too much can lead to tension, fear and resistance.

When the horse is confident over basic cross-country fences, and can cope with undulating ground and gentle slopes, it can be introduced to **drop fences** and **banks.** At first it should be asked to jump up and down small natural banks without an obstacle on top and which it can take in its stride. When the horse has gained confidence, a small obstacle can be placed on the bank. When jumping uphill, i.e. onto the bank, the approach should be ridden at a slightly faster pace, with the horse well 'on the aids'. Drop fences and fences built on a down slope should be approached more slowly, or even in trot.

Cross-country training should always be linked with the horse's basic dressage and jumping training. It should be working at an similar level in each. Making gradual progress in all three elements simultaneously is the only way to develop the horse's suppleness *(Durchlässigkeit)*, agility and controllability. An all-round training prevents the horse from becoming bored and stale and prevents uneven physical wear and tear.

The horse needs to undergo fitness training in order to take part in horse trials or to go out hunting or on long rides. Cross-country work is refreshing for the horse, but it can also be strenuous. It is bad practice, and can be harmful, to suddenly ride the horse hard when it is unfit and unprepared. A good rider can feel when his horse has reached its limits. The horse's formal training should be complemented by hacking it out frequently in order to allow it to relax.

Fitness is developed by steady riding for longish periods in all three gaits. The **canter work** can be gradually increased, with the horse being allowed to trot and walk frequently in between. The speed should be that of a steady working canter,

i.e. about 350-400 metres per minute. Splitting up the canter work, i.e. alternating it with slower work, is more effective for developing the fitness, and also helps to prevent strain on the horse's legs.

Periods of **fast canter** or **sprints** should last for half a minute up to a maximum of a minute to start with, and be followed by a gradual transition back to working canter. Periods of canter should not exceed 3 minutes in all and the horse should only be cantered on fairly level ground.

The **racing gallop** and **steeplechase fences** need only be practised in preparation for three-day events. A suitable track with a hedge and take-off pole across it can be used for this purpose. After a warm-up canter, the horse should be shown the fence to start with and then ridden over it a few times at a slower pace (about 500 metres per minute). The rider should take care to disturb the horse as little as possible. As the training progresses the pace can gradually be increased up to the speed required in the steeplechase phase of the competition (about 600-640 metres per minute). Once the horse has learned to approach the fences in a rhythm and to 'open out' over them, it should not be asked to do this work again unless it is strictly necessary, for example during the build-up to a competition.

Horse trials are considered to be the 'ultimate' equestrian sport. A talented horse is required, and the rider needs to have sensitivity ('feel'), patience and self-control, and to work intensively and conscientiously at the three different elements. The training of an 'eventer' should be especially varied in order to enable it to cope with the different demands of the dressage, show jumping and cross-country.

Brush fence

4.8 Training Horses with Conformation Defects and Difficult Temperaments

Because they have been selectively bred and 'improved', riding horses nowadays are, on the whole, harmoniously built and easy to ride. Poor conformation and difficult temperaments are rare, but when they do occur an experienced trainer and, above all, **patience** are required.

With horses which have **conformation defects** it is particularly important that the horse is loosened up properly before any corrective action is attempted. The best way to do this is usually to lunge or loose-jump the horse, or to take it out on a ride. The same applies to horses which have been badly schooled and which have consequently developed the wrong muscles.

Schooling has very little effect on **defects in conformation of the legs.** However, problems arising from poor conformation of the back can be considerably reduced or even cured completely. A **long back,** especially when it is accompanied by weak loins, makes it more difficult for the horse to step with its hind feet under its centre of gravity. In these horses the hind legs have a dragging action or do not engage sufficiently. The forward thrust and the carrying capacity of the hind legs can be improved by exercises which strengthen the back muscles, especially 'taking the rein forward and down', cavalletti work, and riding up and down hills. In the dressage training, frequent transitions, and so half-halts, can also help to get the horse more 'together'.

A **short back** can make it difficult to attain the requisite degree of suppleness. Often, the horse will collect easily but finds it difficult to bend laterally. Usually the back is stiff, hard and unpleasant to sit on. Also, the horse's legs are subjected to excessive wear and tear. This sort of horse should be ridden in a long outline (but with the head not too low) in order to make it swing through its back as much as possible. Again, long-term schooling over cavalletti, as well as on the flat, will help to improve the horse, as will gymnastic jumping and riding out.

The horse is said to be **croup high** when

its croup is higher than its withers. This conformation defect makes engagement and collection difficult. The rider feels as if he is riding downhill all the time. Here again, long-term gymnastic training will help to teach the horse to bend its hind legs and hindquarter joints more.

Horses which have developed the **wrong muscles in the neck** will also cause problems for the rider. Usually the horse also fails to use its back properly. This fault can normally be cured by systematic schooling and by developing the correct muscles in the neck. It takes time and patience, however. In the hands of an experienced trainer, auxiliary reins can also be useful in the short term.

If the horse keeps trying to throw its head up and hollow its neck while it is being schooled, the trainer can bring the head temporarily slightly behind the vertical. However, he should 'give' with the reins immediately afterwards and push the horse forward until its nose is vertical again. Work on curved tracks (circles and serpentines) is particularly useful for making the horse work more through its back. However, these exercises should not be continued for too long, or they may lead to resistance or even rebellion.

Horses which are **thick through the throat** may have problems bending at the poll and establishing a correct contact.

They should be worked on a long-term basis in an extended outline, until the position of the parotid glands and the lower neck muscles is more acceptable.

> **NOTE**   With problem horses the trainer must always take conformation defects and weaknesses into account. Optimum results will only be achieved if the training is then adapted accordingly.

Temperament problems are often more difficult to cure than problems which result from conformational defects. They are frequently due to incorrect handling and training, for example, the horse has been pushed too hard during its preliminary training or at the beginning of its competitive career. Its excitable, erratic behaviour is then due to fear and insecurity resulting from bad experiences.

If the temperament problem is an acquired one, as opposed to being inborn, closely examining the horse's previous training and handling, and analysing its behaviour, will help the trainer to understand and allay its fears. It will take an experienced trainer to win back the horse's confidence. Likewise, horses with naturally difficult temperaments should only be ridden – if at all – by an experienced, tactful rider.

5 Tips for Riding in Competitions

Taking the horse to shows and taking part in competitions requires careful planning. For **young horses** competition situations contain much that is new, for example, music, spectators and other distractions. It is a good idea to take the horse to a show just to see how it will react. The trainer will then know what he needs to work on.

The **young rider** with no competition experience needs to be carefully prepared for his first show. The horse's behaviour, his own apprehension and the challenge of performing in public can lead to mistakes being made in a competition situation.

Choosing the right competition and the right class is therefore crucial. For the first few competitions it is essential that the rider has plenty of time and a tranquil environment in which to ride in before the competition.

Obviously, whatever the competition, horse and rider must be able to comply with the rules and meet the requirements (see the relevant competition regulations). For the competition to be considered a success, the rider does not necessarily need to win. What is most important is that horse and rider have given as correct and harmonious a performance as their stage of training permits. Everything required in the competition must therefore be practised at home beforehand so that there will be no 'big surprises' on the day. At first the horse and rider should compete at a level below that at which they are training. The level required in the competition will then seem easy and they will not have to cope with difficult exercises as well as the unfamiliar competition situation.

> **NOTE** Practising is done at home, and not in the competition arena.

Riding a dressage test

The horse should be loosened up and prepared before a **dressage test** in the same way that it is ridden in at home, that is, by riding on a loose rein for a long enough period, by performing 'loosening' exercises (*Losgelassenheit*), and by giving the horse sufficient breaks. However, riding-in before the competition should not be overdone or both horse and rider may become tired and lose concentration. The different exercises required in the forthcoming competition should be practised in advance. The requirements will be are laid down in the appropriate rule book and on the test sheets. In the arena, horse and rider must be able to give the test their undivided attention. Ringcraft will be learned later when the rider becomes more experienced.

Competitions serve as a measure of the effectiveness of the day-to-day training. One of the things that is judged is whether the training is on the right lines, that is, basically correct. The judges' notes serve as guidelines for the future training of horse and rider.

Riding in a jumping competition

Before the competition, the rider must walk the course. This will enable him to familiarise himself with the jumps, the combinations and the distances, and to plan the best and most favourable way to ride the course. If the rider is new to competitions, it is essential that the trainer walks the course with him. He will then be able to provide tips and guidelines to help him.

The preparation for the competition should begin with exercises aimed at loosening the horse and getting it well 'on the aids'. Depending on the horse's temperament, keenness and behaviour, the rider can then perhaps jump it over a few low practice fences. Then he can gradually progress to jumping a few fences at competition height, taking care to include frequent breaks for rest and relaxation. How much jumping the horse is asked to do in the practice arena depends on the individual circumstances. Practice jumping should never be overdone or the horse will have nothing left in reserve for the competition.

The horse should enter the arena in trot. After the rider has stopped and saluted in front of the judges (which also serves as an acknowledgement of his acceptance of the rules of the competition), the signal is given to start. The rider then puts the horse onto a large circle and, riding in the light seat, crosses the start in canter, with the appropriate leg leading. The horse should maintain an even, flowing pace throughout. If there is a disagreement between horse and rider between fences or just before a fence, it is essential that the rider remains calm. Charging around and hitting the horse indiscriminately will never produce the desired results.

Turning around after jumping the fence to see if it is still standing is a particularly bad habit. Concentrating on riding correctly at the jump ahead is more important than knowing if faults have occurred at the previous one.

The penalties incurred for knock-downs and refusals, the procedure to be followed after three refusals and the rules and requirements for jumping tests and competitions are laid down in the appropriate rule book.

It goes without saying that the rider should make much of his horse after every round. If the horse has three refusals and is eliminated, the rider is allowed to jump it over another fence before leaving the arena. However, 'sorting the horse out' by means of harsh treatment in the practice arena after an unsuccessful round is a sign of poor horsemanship. Punishing the horse after the event has no educational value and is pointless. Rather, the trainer should see the horse's behaviour as a sign of omissions or faults in the training, which can only be put right by further, systematic schooling.

Riding in cross-country competitions

Before competing in **horse trials,** i.e. **one-, two-** and **three-day events,** horse and rider should undergo lengthy, systematic training in order to develop the necessary fitness. Assuming that the horse has achieved a basic level of fitness and has received an all-round training, approximately six to eight weeks of systematic preparation are needed for a novice level competition.

Before competing in its first horse trial, the horse should already have taken part in dressage and show-jumping competitions, and possibly also in cross-country competitions (hunter trials). The experience gained in these competitions will be of benefit to it and give it confidence in its first one-day event.

The regulations and requirements for horse trials and cross-country competitions are laid down in the rule book of the administering organisation.

When riding-in before the dressage phase, the same principles should apply as in training. However, in horse trials, the trainer needs to consider carefully how intensively the horse should be ridden beforehand, and to decide how long he will need to obtain the necessary degree of 'looseness' *(Losgelassenheit)* in his horse. This will depend on the horse's temperament and level of fitness, and the competition timetable (dressage test on the same day as the cross-country, or the day before). The correct way to remove tension and prepare the horse for the work ahead is usually to spend plenty of time riding it in at a steady pace.

Before the cross-country phase, the rider needs to walk the course. He should then plan in detail and commit to memory the route he is going to take at each obstacle, including any alternative routes, and he should note the positions of any flags. He should also take the going into account. Walking the course for a second time will give the rider another chance to assimilate the details.

The horse should only be given a light meal before the competition and should be allowed enough time to digest it (3-4 hours).

At a one-day event the horse should be ridden-in before the cross-country phase in the same way as for the show jumping. In a three-day event, the first 'roads and tracks' section normally serves to warm the horse up in preparation for the 'steeplechase' section.

As part of the 'tactical' planning of the cross-country test, especially in three-day events, where it consists of several sections, the rider should decide at what pace the different sections should be ridden with that particular horse in order to make the best use of its energies and to divide up the workload in a balanced way. Even within the actual cross-country section, the pace should be varied and carefully planned in order to prevent the horse running out of energy before the end of the course.

For maximum efficiency, the horse should be cantered in a rhythm, the more so since horses try to synchronise their breathing with their canter strides.

During the 10-minute compulsory halt between the second 'roads and tracks' section and the cross-country section, the horse undergoes a veterinary examination. Afterwards it should be led around and kept warm, and rugged up if necessary. The rider should then remount in time to prepare the horse for the cross-country section. Practice jumps are not allowed during the ten minute halt, however.

After the cross-country section, the horse should be led around for long enough to allow the pulse and respiration rates to slow down. It should then be given every care and attention, and provided with water and food in small quantities.

The show-jumping course does not usually present problems. However, it tests the horse's fitness and stamina after the cross-country phase, so the rider needs to bear this in mind when preparing for it. The horse should be cleaned and tidied up for the veterinary examination, after which it should be ridden in quietly in preparation for the jumping. The rider should use basic schooling and 'loosening' exercises to combat any tension or stiffness resulting from the cross-country phase but should avoid overexerting the horse. After suppling it by means of a few practice jumps, the rider can jump the horse over a few – but not many – jumps at competition height. The principles and rules which apply to jumping the course are the same as described above in 'Riding in a Jumping Competition'.

INDEX

Page numbers in *italic* denote illustrations

Also in this series, published by Kenilworth Press

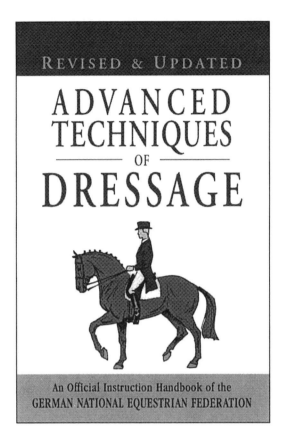

This follow-on teaching manual provides an instruction course in advanced level dressage for horse and rider, using the German training system.

It describes in detail the criteria governing each stage of dressage training – from transitions and extensions to piaffe and passage – giving the aids and training methods to be used for each movement or exercise.

Contents include
The Correct Dressage Seat • Special Tack and Equipment •
The Principles of Training • Transitions and Extensions •
Walk Pirouettes • 'Schaukel' (See-saw) • Shoulder-fore •
Shoulder-in • Travers and Renvers • Half-pass • Flying Changes •
Canter Pirouettes • Piaffe • Passage • Working the Horse in Hand •
Training Problems • Competitions